IN MY HEAD

A NEW APPROACH TO MENTAL WELLNESS

KAPIL GUPTA

ATLANTIC

PUBLISHERS & DISTRIBUTORS (P) LTD

ATLANTIC
PUBLISHERS & DISTRIBUTORS (P) LTD

7/22, Ansari Road, Darya Ganj, New Delhi
Tel.: +91-11-4077 5252, 2327 3880
E-mail: orders@atlanticbooks.com
Web: www.atlanticbooks.com

Published by Atlantic Publishers & Distributors (P) Ltd., 2024

Printed & bound in India by Atlantic Print Services

Advance Praise

Kapil Gupta's *In My Head* is a comprehensive, sustainable and inviting guide to understanding and prioritizing mental health in our day-to-day life, an essential addition to the limited literature that exists on this much-neglected and stigmatized topic in India. Furthermore, Gupta puts forth an urgent call to action to increase the awareness, accessibility, availability, and affordability of mental healthcare in a country where there is an acute shortage of trained professionals and resources in this field.

In short, easy-to-read chapters, Gupta blends a step-by-step approach with a conversational tone, authorial introspection, and unafraid vulnerability. Notably, this systematic guide has a splendid section on neurodiversity, an area that is often misunderstood and inadequately addressed, especially in India. Throughout the book, Gupta invites the reader to explore themes that call for an unguarded examination of the self and argues, most convincingly, that mental healthcare is a universal human right. Using a long-term, holistic outlook and concrete examples, In My Head throws light on the strong connection between a greater focus on mental health and the achievability of the Sustainable Development Goals.

Perhaps the most valuable lesson of this gentle yet meticulous guide is also its simplest and most profound: the only way to find peace is to embrace both the joys and the challenges we confront in life. In My Head shows us how to find equilibrium within the contradictions inherent in the human experience and, at its core, invites us to celebrate life with all its flaws and its grandeur.

Nandana Sen,
Writer, Child-rights activist
and an Award-winning Actor

Kapil Gupta, founder of *Solh Wellness* and a dedicated mental health advocate, unveils the intricate tapestry of mental well-being in *In My Head*. This book serves as a beacon, cutting through misconceptions and stigma surrounding mental health. Kapil's exploration transcends traditional boundaries, urging readers to reconsider their understanding of mental wellness. From the interplay between the economy and mental health to the profound impacts of global challenges, *In My Head* intertwines cause and effect with compassionate narratives. More than a mere exploration, this book is a call to action, reshaping our approach to mental health through the revelation of psychological capital. Drawing from the challenges witnessed during the tumultuous years of COVID-19, Kapil unravels the mysteries of the human psyche, providing tangible solutions and a roadmap to personal empowerment.

As an advisor to Solh, I've witnessed Kapil's unwavering commitment to uncovering personal solutions for mental health challenges. *In My Head* isn't just a book; it's a testament to the transformative potential within each of us. I recommend this book to avid readers seeking a profound understanding of mental health—a valuable resource that enlightens, inspires, and catalyzes positive shifts in perspective on the journey to self-discovery and well-being.

Dr Sravani Reddy G,
Doctorpreneur, Mental Health Advocate
and Humanitarian,
Hyderabad, India

To bring awareness of "mental health" in our society is vital.

Ma Anand Sheela

This wonderful book is groundbreaking, topical, and sincere. The simple yet effective way in which Kapil has explained and demystified mental well-being must be applauded. A must read.

Arjun Hemmady,
Mental Health Campaigner
and Bestselling Author

A revolutionary book on mental health and wellness. Not to be missed!

Kishore Asthana,
President, Mensa Project Dhruv

In My Head simplifies the complex subject of mental health for the layperson. Gupta's '16 Hour Theory' and the 'Power of 5 Adjectives' are particularly impactful. These concepts simplify the understanding of mental health and provide readers with tangible ways to engage with their mental wellness. The metaphorical representation of 'Mann' and 'Demann' to illustrate the dual aspects of our psyche is both creative and relatable, effectively conveying the importance of balance in mental health. Simple explanations. Practical tips

Dr Amit Nagpal,
Founder President, Bloggers Alliance

Kapil Gupta's book *In My Head* is a book at the right time, with the right lens and content and much needed when everyone is suffering from some form of stress, anxiety and mental health issues. Must read for all who want to calm themselves and have a tool kit to be non-judgemental. Through the six sections and the sixth section of creating your own personalised mental health guide. In an age of AI, Kapil's book is about empathy. I enjoyed reading it and it made me think and discover new dimensions of the mental well-being universe.

Dr. Annurag Batra,
Columnist, Author, TV Show Host,
Angel Investor, Serial Entrepreneur,
Founder, exchange4media Group
and Chairman BW Businessworld Group,
and Former Board Member MDI, Gurgaon

Preface

Working in the area of mental health was never something I had planned on pursuing. In fact, since adulthood people have always perceived me as someone with lesser emotions and someone slightly devoid of understanding the depths of stress, anxiety and sadness. While I have found some of this arguable (not that I have argued for them to take me as an emotional person), in reality even I have always found it difficult to understand the pressures that people seem to reflect. I could never lose my sleep over anything or get so depressed that I couldn't laugh or go about my day normally. Upon extensive soul-searching I identified that I have created a new system of gamification for myself, where I can play anything in life as a game (even the question of life-death). Well, more on this at a later point. Let's get back to the topic of the book here.

In the middle of everything that was going on *In My Head* trying to make sense of the world, came COVID. During these unprecedented times of the COVID years (felt like an era), I witnessed the devastating impact it had on people and their well-being - how life was altering for them, situations were getting out of hand, everyone was struggling. While I still had some difficulty seeing myself there, I started to understand what was going on. You could say the frailties of the human head became visible to me. Perhaps, aspects that I had thrown into a bottomless pit came mid-surface. I was able to identify four big stressors that were working against everyone (I call them the 4Cs) and making life difficult. These stressors, as I saw it, were only going to grow bigger with time. At that point, I knew something had to be done.

Add to it the mid-life crisis and a need to do something larger than life, I decided to devote myself to solving this big mystery. And herein came the epiphany that turned it all around. I realized that the reason I have been so good and balanced, and so able to not get too stressed is that I was always working on my mental health. Every action, every decision making, everything that I always did was influenced by my internal ability to think about its impact on my mental health.

It astonished me as I realized that every individual unknowingly does the same. From the food we eat to the people we meet to the sleep we take to whatever activities we engage in, our mental health is the invisible force shaping all our decisions. However, the reason we are unable to get benefitted from it is that we lack the right vocabulary, tools, and framework.

Collective mental well-being is essential not only for personal growth but also for the prosperity of our communities and our economy. The impact of neglected mental health for humanity as a whole is significant losses, hindered progress and lost potential. Fueled by this realization and driven by a desire to make a difference, I founded Solh Wellness. The vision was to create a place where everyone can access the right tools and solutions to take charge of their mental well-being; a place where we can empower individuals with the knowledge and resources they need to flourish.

This book is an extension of that vision. It aims to shed light on the power of our minds and the immense potential that lies within. By understanding and nurturing our mental health, we can unleash a force that propels us towards a brighter, more fulfilling life. Together, let's embark on a journey of self-discovery and growth. Let's equip ourselves with the knowledge and understanding to embrace life's challenges with grace and resilience. This is a book for everyone who seeks to harness their inner strength and unlock the true power within.

Welcome to *In My Head*, where we will explore the depths of our minds and unlock the keys to a healthier, happier, and more empowered life. Let's begin this transformative journey together.

Foreword

In My Head is the book that everyone must have on their bookshelves if they want to learn about various aspects of mental wellness in exquisite yet straightforward ways, be it in terms of exciting vocabulary or engaging illustrations portraying the essence of Mr. Kapil Gupta, who I have known for many years and has been working dedicatedly toward the improvement of mental health worldwide through Solh Wellness. It is a platform that provides a safe space and immense tools for catering to mental wellness needs among all people, whether they are students, employees, or others.

I am happy to see a book exploring mental health's impact on SDGs. The book discusses the 8 SDGs that will be incomplete without a mental health intervention. As an educator and Minister of State for Education in GOI, I must say that Mr Gupta's book is a testament to guiding individuals who face struggles in academics, professional, and even humanitarian fronts caused by a lack of support in their mental health. Such a book can help them recognise their issues and learn how to tackle any hardships that come their way effectively and efficiently.

It is equally applicable to my other Minister of State for External Affairs role for students who go into unfamiliar territories, leaving their homes and people who do. In my home territory in the Northeast, there has been a worrisome and deteriorating trend in mental wellness, which such books and initiatives can help.

The book makes understanding mental health easier. It is a complete guide and even a 'to your face,' as it unties many knots and hits you with hard truths that you have been hiding or ignoring, even to yourself. *In My Head* can make you feel many emotions but with the right proportion of logic, humour, and sensibility. So, be ready to face everything and anything before choosing this book.

Dr. Rajkumar Ranjan Singh,
Minister of State for Education and
External Affairs, Government of India,
Author, Teacher and Researcher

Acknowledgements

This book is a result of a countless number of hours spent on understanding, talking, creating, and spreading mental wellness. It started with an epiphany and resulted into this book and a life mission. This book was an afterthought of working on Solh Wellness, a uniquely positioned mental wellness platform looking to fulfil the mission of mental wellness as a universal human right.

However, it would not have been complete without the diligence and hard work of the countless people who have worked with me over the years. People have come and gone, but their contribution cannot be stated enough. Special mention must go to Muskan, Navita, Kavya, Shivani, Preeti, Drishti, Ritika, Dipna, Mansi, Aman, Waseem, Atishay, and last but not least, Dr Tarun Sehgal for helping me fulfil this mission. A special thank you to my friend and Publisher, Manish Gupta (Atlantic Publishers), for his support as well.

I have shared the book manuscript with numerous people and have received some wonderful feedback. I want to thank them all for their kind words, too. Some of that feedback is going in print as well.

Thank you must be said to those who have given me all the good, bad, and ugly experiences over the last few years that have given me the power, the wisdom, and the vision to write this. Thank you to these sane and, insane, and brilliant people in my life. Finally, thanks to all the readers. Please connect with me @kapgup - let's keep the conversation going.

Contents

Preface vii
Foreword ix
Acknowledgements xi

SECTION I

Introduction

1. What is Mental Health? 3
2. The Power of the 5 Adjectives 7
3. Quantifying Mental Health with PsyCap 11

SECTION II

Problems

1. Bridging the Gap: Vocabulary, Tools, and Framework 17
   Vocabulary 18
   Tools 19
   Framework 20
2. The 4Cs of Mental Health 21
   Climate 23
   Conflict 25
   Conformity 27
   Contagion 29
3. The Quest for Objectivity in Diagnosis and Treatment 31
4. The Present and Future Implications of the Downward Spiral 37
5. Ending the Hush-Hush: Removing the Stigma 41

6. Structural and Financial Barriers in Mental Health 45

7. Pandemic Within the Pandemic: How COVID-19 Catalyzed Mental Health 49

SECTION III

Solutions

1. The Path to Mental Wellness: 5 Milestones 55

2. The Power of Early Intervention 59

3. Thriving Basics: Eat, Sleep, Move, Breathe, Hydrate 65

4. The Healing Power of Words: The Connection Between Readership, Authorship, and Mental Health 69

5. Happiness, Peace, and Being Passionately Unattached 73

6. Holistic Healing: Complementary Therapies for Mental Well-being 77

7. Spirituality and Religion: The Social Solutions for Mental Health 81

8. Developing and Recovering PsyCap: Get Your Mental Money Back 85

9. Revolutionizing Mental Health: Harnessing the Power of Digital Technology 89

SECTION IV

Solh

1. The Solh Way 97

2. A Personalized and Comprehensive Approach to Mental Health 101

3. Tools and Solutions 103

Self-Help 103
Community Support 105
Expert Services 108

4. Mental Health is a Universal Human Right 111

5. Sustainability: Embracing Mental Wellness as a Way of Life 115

SECTION V

SDGs & Mental Wellness

1. Mental Wellness & SDG 1: No Poverty 121
2. Mental Wellness & SDG 3: Good Health & Well-Being 123
3. Mental Wellness & SDG 4: Quality Education 127
4. Mental Wellness & SDG 5: Gender Equality 131
5. Mental Wellness & SDG 8: Decent Work & Economic Growth 135
6. Mental Wellness & SDG 10: Reduced Inequalities 139
7. Mental Wellness & SDG 11: Sustainable Cities and Communities 141
8. Mental Wellness & SDG 13: Climate Action 143

SECTION VI

Your Mental Health Guide

1. Psychotic and Neurotic Disorders: Understanding Common Mental Health Issues 147
2. Understanding Therapy and Medication 151
3. Who To Call?: Different Professionals and When To Turn To Them 155
4. Neurodiversity and Neuro-Inclusivity 161
5. Exploring Neuro-Developmental Disorders 167
Autism Spectrum Disorder (ASD) 167
Learning Disabilities (LD) 172
Attention Deficit Hyperactivity Disorder (ADHD) 175

Conclusion 183

About the Author 191

Section I

INTRODUCTION

1
What is Mental Health?

"All our actions and decisions are driven to optimize mental health. I call this the '16-Hour Theory'."

Before we begin our journey towards better mental health, we need to understand some basic concepts. First and foremost - what is mental health? If I put you and 9 other people on the spot and ask you this question, I'm sure that your definition of mental health won't match the definition given by others. Every person will define it in a way that fits their own self, in terms of what works for them.

I have done this exercise with thousands of people during numerous workshops. The prompt is always the same - what do you do for your mental health? Some come back with a vehement 'nothing'. Others name some activity they engage in (yoga, meditation, gym, travel, cooking, some kind of performing arts, etc.), or that they have been to a counselor or a therapist in the past. Yet almost no one thinks of what I call the **'16 Hour Theory'**. I believe that for more than 16 hours in a day everyday, all that we do is mental health - from the food we eat, to the people we meet, and the places that we go to. We all are working towards our mental health in our daily routine, each day, knowingly or unknowingly. It is just a matter of knowing the right vocabulary, tools and framework that we can work towards our mental health with more efficiency. We will talk more about this in the next section.

Coming back to the definition of mental health — a good starting point would be to keep all subjectivity aside and agree on some basics before we move forward. In a nutshell, mental health is the "overall well-being of the emotional, psychological and social state of mind - what is called the state of balance or disbalance between the mind, body, soul and spirit". It involves a person's ability to think, feel and act, and determines how well a person can handle challenges and navigate life's obstacles. Now let's bring in the subjective element - understanding mental health becomes more complex in real life simply because the human experience is so varied and there are too many factors at play. Every mindset is different and each individual has their own unique stimuli that work for their mental health. The process of how each individual works towards their mental health is also different. For some people, taking a break or sleeping some extra hours is a way to enhance mental health. For others, putting in extra hours into their work or crossing things off their checklist is a way to better mental health. While both ways are very different, they are equally as effective depending on what works well for the person following them.

We can understand the concept of mental health and how it affects people on individual levels in a better way through Mann and Demann - let me introduce you to them!

Mann is presented in an angelic form with a halo and is the ever effervescent side of our personality - chirpy, cool and carefree - with an optimistic mindset and readiness to face challenges. Mann is proactive and takes action to accomplish tasks efficiently and effectively. Demann, presented in a demonic form with devil's horns, is the other side of the coin - pessimistic, fearful and careful - symbolizing the human tendency to focus on problems and obstacles. Demann procrastinates and delays the completion of simple tasks, often causing unnecessary stress and hindering progress. Mann understands where Demann's inhibitions are coming from, and never lets go of his little friend. Demann uses these inhibitions to protect Mann and helps him stay grounded. In this way, they both are necessary for each other's survival and become an indispensable part of us.

The characters of Mann and Demann serve as broader representations of human tendencies and attitudes. They can be seen as a metaphor for the eternal struggle that we all face in life between positivity and negativity. The idea is to view

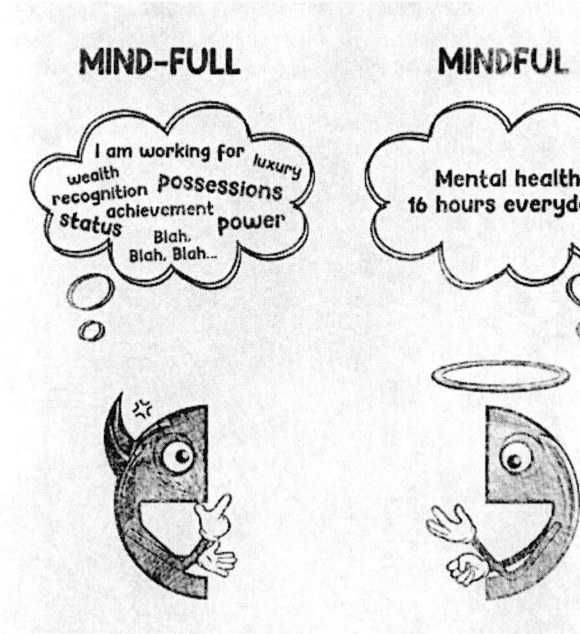

Figure 1

the two sides of the human psyche as good and bad, with both being an integral part of it.

The lesson to be learnt from Mann and Demann is simple - mental health is all about balance. Happiness and sadness are part of life and we need to accept them both to be able to live a peaceful life. The goal should not be to chase happiness, it should be to find happiness along the way, while also embracing the not so happy moments. As we navigate this nuanced path, let us remember that mental health is a journey, where embracing both happiness and challenges paves the way for a fulfilling life.

2

The Power of the 5 Adjectives

"Mental Health for Dummies: The 5 adjectives."

One of the key challenges in the pursuit of mental health is the lack of biomarkers, which makes mental health extremely complicated and obscure. There are 8 billion ways in which people's mental health works (simply because the current human population is 8 billion), and humans discover newer ways to tackle their daily challenges every day. In order to understand mental health more deeply, I have simplified it into 5 adjectives. Experts will dislike this simplification and it is certainly not meant to be clinically correct. However, in all my experience, this works for an easy grasp for most people.

In my view, mental health consists of three things that people work to reduce (I call them the 'Demann' adjectives) and two that they work to increase (the 'Mann' adjectives). Demann grapples with being Sad, Lonely and Stressed, while Mann experiences being Happy and at Peace. Every aspect of human emotion can be simplified within this easy to understand classification.

In daily activities, any or all of these adjectives are involved. If a person goes through a day without experiencing them, it means they have merely existed rather than truly lived. If our mental health is affected for good or bad, then either one or all of these five adjectives are accountable for that. While people want to abolish Sadness, Loneliness and Stress, in reality that will make life lose its meaning. The ongoing pursuit to move from the Demann state to a Mann state is how I define life. As simple as that. You could even consider and create it as a game for yourself.

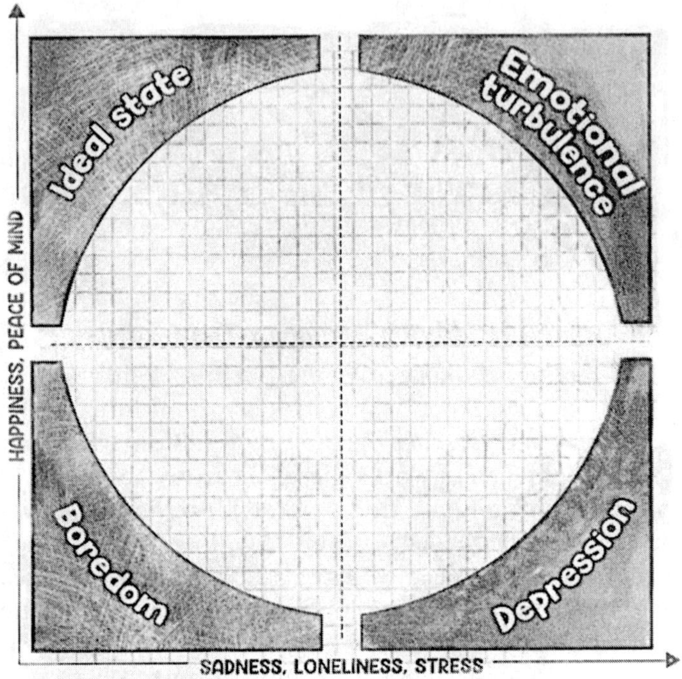

Figure 2

These adjectives can be a roller coaster ride in day-to-day life, such as experiencing excessive happiness or being overwhelmed by stress. Tackling these five adjectives can balance our mental health. Along with expanding happiness and peace of mind, minimizing sadness, loneliness, and stress can boost mental wellness. Every individual should strive to work on these adjectives because such efforts contribute to a balanced and improved mental health, allowing for increased productivity and a happier life. This story will help you understand these adjectives better:

In my office, two interns joined at the same time, named Mann and Demann. After three months, I conducted a meeting where I confirmed Mann's job and increased his salary, while I encouraged Demann to try harder next time. The minute after my decision, Mann and Demann asked about the thought behind it.

I went on to explain that Mann had good connections with everyone in the office. He enjoyed lunch with his friends, cracked jokes while working, and listened to music whenever he got a break from work. He either meditated or spent some peaceful time with his friends, which allowed him to experience happiness and peace. Consequently, he became more productive and contributed his best to the office. On the contrary, Demann used to come to the office but didn't make friends and stayed alone the whole day. He was left with a sense of loneliness, sadness and stress, which reflected in his work and negatively impacted his performance, preventing him from giving his best.

After the meeting, Demann understood that sadness, loneliness, and stress deteriorate mental health, while happiness and peace of mind have a positive impact on mental well-being, enabling an individual to live a better and happier life.

Through the above story, we can see the five adjectives in action. In the intricate tapestry of human emotions and experiences, referencing such simplified frameworks can prove to be of great help.

3

Quantifying Mental Health with PsyCap

"PsyCap is the smart deposit for your most precious asset: Mental Health."

The term Psychological Capital or PsyCap was originally coined in 2004 by Fred Luthans. The concept was designed for usage in organizations, with its four pillars: Hope, Efficacy, Resilience and Optimism. However, what I refer to as PsyCap here is slightly different.

My idea behind psychological capital is that every action we take towards improving our mental health contributes to the accumulation of a "currency." Similar to how we accumulate wealth by saving money, we can accumulate psychological capital by investing in activities and practices that enhance our well-being.

Let me explain - in a day, we undertake many activities, and all of these activities bear an outcome for our mental health. If we were to track all these activities, and create a point system where rewards are given for activities bearing positive results, then we can build our own psychological capital measurement system. What benefit would this have? Consciously working towards increasing our PsyCap points can gradually improve our mental health. It will allow us to track our progress and gain insights into our mental health journey and motivate individuals to invest more in their mental health. As they witness the growth of their psychological capital over time, it will create a positive feedback loop.

Figure 3

The benefits of PsyCap go beyond the personal level and have broader societal and economic implications. Mental health issues, like depression, anxiety, and burnout, are a leading cause of the lost productivity worldwide. This has a significant impact on individuals, families, and communities, as well as on the economy as a whole. People with higher levels of psychological capital are better equipped to manage stress and cope with these challenges. They are also more likely to have positive relationships with others. But it doesn't end here - psychological capital is a resource that can be shared and leveraged across different individuals and contexts. It can be generated by anyone, regardless of their background, circumstances, or resources, and at any point of their life. It is not something that can be bought or acquired, but rather something that needs to be cultivated through intentional effort and hard work.

At its core, psychological capital is about building resilience and a sense of purpose and control over one's life. In contrast to monetary capital, which is finite and can only be used by a particular individual once, psychological capital is an infinitely renewable resource that can benefit multiple individuals over time. When one person invests in their mental wellness and builds their psychological capital, the positive impact can ripple out to others in their social networks and beyond. For example, when a leader or mentor exhibits strong psychological capital, it inspires and motivates those around them to do the same. Similarly, when people work together to promote mental wellness, they can create a culture of support and empowerment that benefits everyone.

Successful people use their psychological capital resources to overcome obstacles and accomplish their objectives. Elon Musk exhibits hope and tenacity by persevering in his endeavors despite failures. Oprah Winfrey is an example of optimism and self-efficacy. J.K. Rowling overcame rejection thanks to her optimism and resilience, which allowed her to create the adored Harry Potter series. Nelson Mandela was a shining example of fortitude and optimism, effectively reshaping South Africa with his unflinching faith in peace. These are just a few examples of how psychological capital enables people to overcome challenges, maintain motivation, and live satisfying lives even in the face of difficulty.

Section II

PROBLEMS

1

Bridging the Gap: Vocabulary, Tools, and Framework

"The mental wellness trifecta we need but don't get: Vocabulary, Tools, and Framework."

Mental health is probably the most tabooed subject in human conversations. It is something that should be talked about more, yet it is often neglected and stigmatized in society. For those who suffer from mental health related problems, it can be challenging to find the courage to speak up and seek help due to the fear of being judged or discriminated against. This can create a sense of isolation and shame, leading to further mental health issues, and the cycle goes on and on with no end in sight. As we have developed as a society, the stigma is getting reduced albeit slowly. Even if you are the more empowered, more liberal one, it simply means you will be comfortable with other people talking about their mental health. It is still an extremely difficult subject for people when they have to talk about themselves.

We discussed the 16-hour theory in the previous section where we talked about how everyone works on their mental health all-day, everyday. The food you eat, the people you meet, the places that you go to, it's all about your mental health. If we can all be empowered to look at our lives that way, the immediate reaction will be firstly for the stigma around mental health to disappear, and secondly for people to be able to self-sustain this part of their life. If you could just start looking at everything in your life from the lens of mental health!

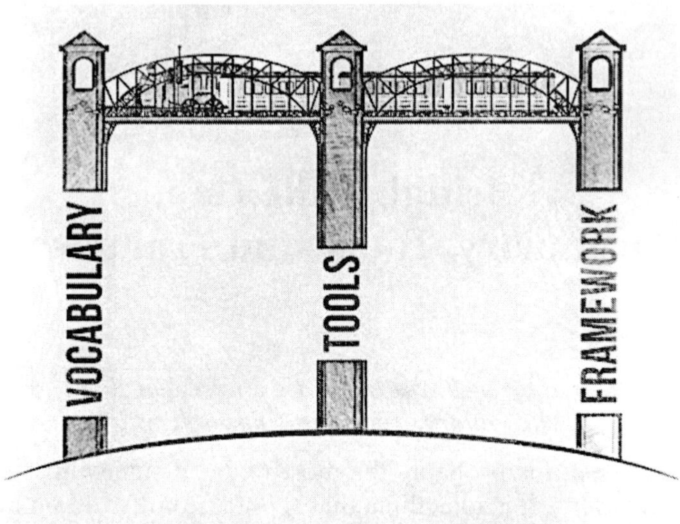

Figure 4

So, the next logical question is - what prevents you from doing that? In my view, the problem is a lack of **Vocabulary** (the words to describe our mental health), **Tools** (ways to work on our mental health) and **Framework** (system in which to work on our mental health). Let me walk you through all three of these one by one.

Vocabulary

The vocabulary of mental health consists of elements discussed in the first section. It consists of the 16 hour theory, that is being aware that everything you do in your life is driven by mental health. Another component is the simplification of mental health into easy to understand and easy to use terms. I have done this with the 5 adjectives (sadness, loneliness, stress, happiness and peace of mind).

The language we use in our daily life affects the way we act and react to situations. If I am feeling exhausted, but the word I use to describe it is angry, it changes the meaning, and also ends up impacting the way I will act on this feeling. This is just an example of how using the wrong words to describe something can have a negative outcome. People make mistakes like this in their daily life, and it has big impacts on their mental health.

To address this issue, knowing the right vocabulary is important. A shift in language is much needed to represent a growing understanding of the importance of mental health and well-being in our society. By promoting a more empowering view of mental health, we can help to reduce the stigma and make it easier for individuals to seek help and support.

Tools

Taking care of our mental health is essential for leading a healthy and fulfilling life. Even with the right vocabulary, there will certainly be support needed for the times when you are sad, stressed or lonely. I categorize the tools that can help us improve our mental well-being into three parts: self-help, community, and professional services.

Self-help refers to the steps we take to improve our mental health on our own, without the involvement of other people. For me, it is pursuing what stimulates you, engaging in hobbies that bring joy and fulfillment. Depending on your preferences, this could include activities like exercising, eating a healthy diet, and getting enough sleep, along with more specific activities like performing arts or activities to work directly on your mental health such as practicing relaxation techniques. Self-help can also include reading books, articles, and blogs about mental health, and using apps and online resources that provide guidance on how to manage stress, anxiety, and other mental health issues. They should be an inclusion in everyone's daily lives.

Community support involves seeking guidance and support from family, friends, and other members of one's social network. This can include simply talking to a trusted friend or family member about your struggles or joining communities like support groups. The basic idea is to create a safe and inclusive environment where people feel comfortable talking about their mental health issues without fear of judgment or stigma. Since it's mental health and we are talking about the deeply buried thoughts and emotions, anonymity is usually appreciated, which makes support groups popular.

Professional services refer to the specialized help and support provided by mental health professionals, such as therapists, psychiatrists, and psychologists. Professionals are trained to provide a range of services, including therapy, medication, and other interventions which are not only effective in serious mental health issues but can also be used for self-growth. Mental health professionals remain an indispensable part of the mental health ecosystem.

Framework

The societal structure that we live in today has been shaped by centuries of traditions and beliefs. While many aspects of this structure have brought us progress and prosperity, there are also parts of it that are not useful anymore. One such area that has turned void is mental health.

For too long, mental health has been a taboo subject, swept under the rug and hidden away from public discussion. This has led to a society that stigmatizes mental illness and often fails to provide adequate support for those who are struggling. However, it is becoming increasingly clear that we cannot continue to ignore the topic if we want to create a society that truly supports the well-being of all its members.

To remove the stigma, we need to work towards creating a societal framework that prioritizes mental health. One important step to be taken towards this is to generate conversations around mental health and normalize talking about it. This will help familiarize people with mental illnesses and create more acceptance and support. Another way is to raise awareness about the importance of good mental health in different areas, such as the workplace, schools, home, etc.

By educating people on the topic of mental health and the tools available to improve it, accompanied by the right vocabulary and framework, we can create a happier and healthier society where people are empowered to take charge of their mental well-being.

2

The 4Cs of Mental Health

"From problem to pandemic: 4Cs changing mental wellness."

In the fast-paced and ever-changing world we live in, our lives have always been impacted by new challenges. However, COVID has caused a complete upheaval and topsy-turvy in the society. Terms like lockdown, isolation, travel restrictions, and closed borders have become part of our daily vocabulary, symbolizing the significant shifts we have experienced. These turbulent times have given rise to a multitude of challenges that affect our mental well-being. In this chapter, we will explore some of the prominent challenges we face, including the impact of the COVID pandemic, the consequences of the digital lifestyle, the breakdown of extended support structures, and the vulnerabilities of the younger generation. Additionally, we will discuss the need for a focus on preventive mental health care and the role of governments in addressing these issues.

The COVID Impact - Rise of Stress

The COVID-19 pandemic has brought unprecedented challenges, leaving no aspect of life untouched. The constant fear of contracting the virus, loss of loved ones, economic uncertainties, and the disruption of daily routines have collectively led to increased stress levels among individuals and communities. The pandemic's toll on mental health has been profound, and addressing this crisis has become imperative.

The Digital Lifestyle - Affecting Social Skills

The advent of technology and the digital era has transformed the way we live and interact with others. While it has connected us globally, the digital lifestyle has also caused issues in developing and maintaining meaningful social skills.

Nuclear Families - The Absence of Extended Support

Traditional extended support structures, once prevalent in communities, have diminished with the rise of nuclear families. The lack of extended family support can create a sense of isolation, especially during challenging times.

The Younger Generation - Bearing the Brunt

The younger generation faces unique challenges amidst the turbulence of today's world. Their lives are deeply impacted by societal changes, academic pressures, economic uncertainties, and the influence of digital media. These factors, coupled with the limited availability of emotional support, leave them particularly vulnerable to mental health struggles.

Lack of Focus on Preventive Care

While addressing higher-level mental health disorders is crucial, there is an equally significant need to prioritize preventive care. Educating individuals about mental well-being, promoting resilience-building strategies, and fostering open dialogue about mental health are essential in cultivating a proactive approach to mental wellness.

The Role of Government

Governments play a critical role in addressing mental health challenges in turbulent times. Allocating resources for mental health services, promoting mental health awareness campaigns, and integrating mental health into healthcare systems are vital steps to ensure the well-being of their citizens.

While these are some factors that are affecting the mental health of people today, I now want to talk about some other extremely important factors which have a much broader influence in today's world. I refer to these four factors as the 4Cs of mental health. These are Climate, Conflict, Conformity, and Contagion. Let's talk about them.

Figure 5

Climate

Climate or weather is the first factor I will talk about that affects mental health. You may have rarely observed the extent to which climate can have an impact on someone's mental well-being. Increasing change in climate is leading to a rise in mental health problems among a notable population, causing it to collapse and become imbalanced. From climate-induced stress arising from pollution and lifestyle choices to worries about the future of ourselves and the planet, extreme weather patterns, and the stress of overpopulation in urban areas, let's examine how climate change takes a toll on our mental health.

Climate-Induced Stress

Climate change triggers stress through various interconnected factors:

Pollution and Lifestyle: The consequences of pollution and unsustainable lifestyles weigh heavily on our minds. Air and water pollution, exacerbated by human activities, contribute to a sense of environmental vulnerability and health concerns, increasing stress levels.

Changing Climate and Anxiety: The shifting weather patterns, such as unexpected rainfall, droughts, storms, and floods, create a sense of unpredictability and insecurity, causing anxiety among communities living in affected regions.

Worry About the Future

The uncertainty and potential consequences of climate change lead to profound worries:

Personal Concerns: Worries about the future's environmental challenges, such as limited access to clean drinking water and sufficient food, create anxiety about personal well-being and survival.

Global Impact: The broader implications of climate change on a global scale, including rising sea levels and extreme weather events, contribute to feelings of powerlessness and distress about the fate of the planet and future generations.

Extreme Weather Patterns

The intensifying weather events due to climate change have severe psychological implications:

Trauma and Fear: Experiencing or witnessing extreme weather events like hurricanes, wildfires, and other natural disasters can cause trauma, fear, and even post-traumatic stress disorder (PTSD).

Loss and Grief: Natural disasters result in the loss of lives, homes, and livelihoods, leading to grief and emotional distress for the affected individuals and communities.

Overpopulation and Urban Stress

The strain of overpopulation in urban areas adds another layer of stress:

Urban Stress: Overcrowded cities often face problems related to competition for resources, employment, and housing, which contribute to mental health challenges.

Depletion of Natural Spaces: Urbanization results in a loss of green spaces and natural environments, impacting mental well-being by reducing opportunities for relaxation and connection with nature.

Conclusion

Climate change, with its complex web of impacts, significantly affects our mental health. Climate-induced stress from pollution and lifestyle choices, coupled with worries about the future, create anxiety about personal well-being and the fate of our planet. Extreme weather events cause trauma, fear, and grief in affected communities. Moreover, overpopulation and urban stress add further strain on mental well-being. Recognizing the interplay between climate change and mental health is crucial for developing effective strategies to address these challenges.

As we navigate the complexities of climate change, collective action and individual efforts to mitigate its impacts are essential. Prioritizing mental health support and resilience-building strategies can help individuals and communities cope with the psychological toll of climate change. Together, by acknowledging and addressing the psychological aspects of climate change, we can work towards a more resilient and compassionate world for current and future generations.

Conflict

Conflict, a clash resulting from opposing interests, beliefs, or actions, is an inherent part of the human experience. Let's examine how conflict impacts mental health, affecting individuals and societies on various levels, and explore ways to navigate these challenges.

Geopolitical Tensions

Geopolitical tensions occur when countries or regions have differing interests or ideologies, leading to disputes and hostilities. These tensions can significantly impact mental well-being:

Fear and Uncertainty: Heightened geopolitical tensions create an atmosphere of fear and uncertainty among populations. Citizens may worry about their safety and the potential consequences of escalating conflicts.

Social Divisions: Geopolitical tensions can lead to divisions within societies, causing rifts between communities and ethnic groups, which may result in increased social stress and anxiety.

Displacement and Refugees: Protracted geopolitical conflicts often force people to leave their homes, becoming refugees. Such displacement leads to trauma, grief, and mental health challenges for those affected.

Wars - An Increasingly Global Phenomenon

Modern warfare has transcended national borders, becoming a global issue with profound mental health implications:

Trauma and PTSD: Those directly involved in wars, such as soldiers and civilians living in conflict zones, often experience trauma and post-traumatic stress disorder (PTSD) due to exposure to violence and atrocities.

Secondary Trauma: Wars affect not only those directly involved but also their families and loved ones. Witnessing the physical and emotional toll of war on their close ones can lead to secondary trauma and mental health struggles.

Global Witnessing: In the digital age, people worldwide can witness the horrors of wars through media coverage. Constant exposure to violence and suffering can contribute to collective feelings of helplessness and emotional distress.

Everyday Conflicts Due to Changing Life Dynamics

As societies evolve and adapt to changing circumstances, everyday conflicts can arise from various sources:

Social and Cultural Shifts: Rapid societal changes can lead to conflicts between generations or differing cultural norms, causing stress and strain in families and communities.

Economic Struggles: Financial hardships and economic disparities can lead to conflicts related to job security, financial stability, and access to resources.

Lifestyle Changes: The fast-paced nature of modern life can result in conflicts arising from work-life balance, personal relationships, and mental health management.

Conclusion

Conflict, in its various forms, has a profound impact on mental health, affecting individuals and societies alike. Geopolitical tensions create fear and uncertainty, while wars bring trauma and suffering on a global scale. Everyday conflicts arising from changing life dynamics can lead to personal struggles and societal stress. To navigate these challenges, fostering empathy, promoting dialogue, and seeking peaceful resolutions are crucial. Providing mental health support and resources to those affected by conflict is equally important. By recognizing the interconnectedness of mental well-being and conflict resolution, we can pave the way for a more compassionate, harmonious world where the burden of conflict on mental health is eased.

Conformity

Conformity is the tendency for an individual to align their attitudes, beliefs, and behaviors with those of the people around them. This phenomenon is driven by internal expectations individuals place on themselves and external pressures imposed by family, peers, and society. The desire to carve out a place in the world or gain acceptance often leads people to indulge in conformity, which can have profound consequences on mental health.

Expectations from Self

Internal expectations play a significant role in conformity. As humans, we are social beings, and our desire for acceptance and belonging drives us to adopt certain behaviors and attitudes that we perceive as conducive to fitting in. In pursuing societal norms and personal aspirations, individuals may set high standards for themselves, believing that conforming to these ideals will lead to greater happiness and fulfillment. They might start emulating certain behaviors, adopting specific attitudes, or modifying their lifestyles to align with what they believe to be the norm, even if it means sacrificing aspects of their authentic selves.

Expectations from Others

People often conform to social groups or adopt certain behaviors to gain acceptance, approval, or validation from those they interact with regularly. The need to feel a sense of belonging can lead individuals to assimilate into particular social circles, even if it means compromising their values or personal preferences. The fear of rejection or social exclusion can be powerful motivators, compelling people to change their authentic selves to gain acceptance and approval. Friends, for instance, may influence individuals to adopt certain behaviors or habits, while family members might have strong beliefs that they expect everyone in the family to follow.

Conclusion

While conformity may provide short-term feelings of acceptance and belonging, the constant struggle to maintain this facade can take a toll on mental well-being. Many individuals find themselves experiencing stress and anxiety because they are not genuinely driven to make these changes, but rather feel compelled to do so to meet societal expectations. The conflict between the desire for acceptance and the need to stay true to oneself can lead to feelings of disconnection and may even escalate into more serious problems.

It is essential to strike a balance between personal growth and authenticity. While change is a natural part of life, it should come from within and align with one's values and genuine aspirations. By recognizing the influence of conformity, individuals can make mindful choices that promote mental well-being and preserve their authenticity. Embracing one's unique qualities and values can lead to a more fulfilling and meaningful life, free from the constant struggle to conform to external expectations.

Contagion

In recent times, the world has witnessed the devastating impact of contagion, particularly through the COVID-19 pandemic. Beyond physical health, these contagious illnesses have deeply affected mental health, causing widespread distress, fear, and uncertainty. This influence of contagion on mental well-being comprises two key aspects - the impact of physical illness on mental health, and the fear of disease contraction. Let's take a look at them.

Impact of Physical Illness on Mental Health

When a person falls victim to a physical illness, the repercussions are not limited to the body alone. The toll on mental health can be equally significant, not only for the patient but also for their family and loved ones.

Emotional Turmoil: Coping with physical symptoms and limitations can lead to emotional distress, including anxiety, sadness, frustration, and even depression.

Uncertainty and Fear: The uncertainty surrounding the course of the illness and the potential outcomes can exacerbate fear and anxiety, making it challenging to maintain a positive outlook.

Burden of Dependency: Those facing severe physical illnesses may become dependent on others for care, leading to feelings of helplessness and loss of control over their lives.

Social Isolation: Stigmatization and fear of contagion can lead to social isolation and withdrawal from friends and family, further impacting mental well-being.

Impact of the Fear of Illness on Mental Health

The fear of contracting a contagious disease can be as detrimental to mental health as the illness itself. The COVID-19 pandemic serves as an exemplar of how widespread fear can profoundly affect mental well-being:

Heightened Anxiety: Constant exposure to news and updates about illness can fuel anxiety.

Pandemic Fatigue: Long-term fear and uncertainty can lead to a sense of emotional exhaustion and detachment from self-care.

Grief and Loss: The fear of illness may be compounded by the loss of loved ones, further impacting mental health by triggering grief and bereavement.

Isolation and Lockdown-Induced Stress

To curb the spread of contagious diseases, measures such as isolation and lockdowns are implemented. However, these necessary precautions have unintended consequences on mental health:

Loneliness: Prolonged periods of isolation can lead to feelings of loneliness, which have been linked to increased rates of depression and anxiety.

Disrupted Routine: The disruption of daily routines can cause stress, as individuals struggle to adapt to a new way of life, affecting their sense of purpose and stability.

Financial Strain: The economic repercussions of lockdowns can lead to financial stress and anxiety, adding to the mental health burden.

Conclusion

Contagion, be it in terms of the physical illness itself or the fear of contracting it, poses a significant threat to mental health. The COVID-19 pandemic has shown us how interconnected our physical and mental well-being truly is. As we move forward, it is essential to prioritize mental health support alongside physical health measures during contagions. Providing education, destigmatizing mental health, and fostering social connections can help individuals and communities cope better with the psychological impact of contagious illnesses.

Together, we can build resilience and navigate these challenges with greater strength and understanding.

3

The Quest for Objectivity in Diagnosis and Treatment

"Love, hate and mental health: 3 things that can't be measured."

Mental health disorders affect millions of people worldwide. They can take a major toll on a person's well-being and at times, need the support of medications in congruence with therapy for their treatment. Despite the growing recognition of mental health as a global health priority, developing effective medications for mental disorders remains a complex and multifaceted endeavor that not much research has been done on. Medications are an integral part of many areas of treatment, but they have their downfalls.

Everyone has different experiences when it comes to mental health related issues. We all perceive things differently and react to things differently. Therefore, the treatment approaches used also vary from person to person. There is no objectivity or standardization of treatment because every person experiences different symptoms for a specific issue. For instance, two people suffering from anxiety do not compulsorily experience the same symptoms. One person might experience dizziness and restlessness, and another might have stomach aches and feel nauseous, but both are manifestations of anxiety. Let's talk about some challenges that arise when we talk about medicine usage in the world of psychiatry.

Limited Biomarkers for Diagnosis and Treatment

Mental health disorders often lack definitive biomarkers for accurate diagnosis and treatment monitoring. Even though the

DSM-5 does mention criteria for diagnosis of each disorder, there is still a lot of room for subjectivity involved. Diagnosis for a huge part depends on the person's reported experiences, which cannot be objectively verified. The absence of objective measures to assess treatment responses makes it challenging to demonstrate the efficacy of potential medications in clinical trials. The development of biomarkers is crucial to ensure early detection, targeted treatment, and personalized care for patients.

Figure 6

Variability in Symptoms and Treatments

'Symptoms' refer to the indicators that suggest the presence of a mental disorder or condition. These symptoms can be behavioral, emotional, cognitive, or physical in nature and are typically assessed by mental health professionals to diagnose and understand an individual's mental health status. Every disorder or illness has different symptoms that define it and yet these are not fixed. It means that every person presents different symptoms, which makes diagnosis tricky.

A similar pattern is seen in treatment as well - not every drug works for every individual. Therefore, finding the right dosage of a particular medication and seeing if the medication is effective or not becomes a trial and error process.

Effectiveness vs Side-Effects

The side-effects of medications used to treat various mental health issues can vary depending on the specific medication and individual response. It's important to note that not everyone will experience the same side-effects, and some individuals may not experience any side-effects at all. In some cases, the benefits of medication in managing mental health conditions may outweigh the potential side-effects.

For instance, in cases of depression, individuals are commonly prescribed with Selective Serotonin Reuptake Inhibitors (SSRIs) that may cause side-effects such as nausea, insomnia, drowsiness, and sexual dysfunction, but that does not mean every person taking SSRIs will face such side-effects. The effectiveness of any medication can only be known after its consumption. It's crucial to work closely with a healthcare professional when starting or adjusting medications for mental health issues.

Ethical Considerations and Research and Development Costs

Psychiatric drug development trials are known to have one of the lowest success rates. Testing medications for checking their effectiveness can involve ethical considerations. It is risky because medication trials on subjects or patients can lead to possible complications, such as risk of worsening illness due to ineffective medicines or placebos. This leads to a lack of research and development of effective medicines, especially when it comes to mental health.

Problems in the Indian Context

Shortage of Professionals

As per research from the Indian Journal of Psychiatry, India has 0.75 psychiatrists and psychologists per 100,000 people. India requires 13,500 psychiatrists and 20,250 clinical psychologists but only 3,800 psychiatrists and 900 clinical psychologists are present in mental healthcare services, according to the Ministry of Health and Family Welfare.

Such statistics show the condition of mental health facilities in our country and how much it needs to improve. Such a shortage of professionals and lack of awareness creates more stigma around mental health in people, further worsening the situation.

Reliance on Faith Healers

In a country like India, everyone has their own beliefs and faith, but such ideas stop people from seeking help for mental health issues timely. For most people, their primary stop for 'gaining peace & stability' is faith healers, such as Babas. Such healers are believed to be able to provide cures for life's problems, but when the causality comes from something that needs clinical attention, it becomes a roadblock that stops people from seeking timely help. When the condition becomes extreme is when people seek professional help. In such a scenario, the clinician often has no other option but to prescribe medications to the patient.

Focus on Physical Symptoms

In our country, people tend to focus more on the physical symptoms that they experience compared to their feelings and thoughts. People also tend to report their physical experiences more, for example, someone who might be feeling anxious is more likely to talk about their somatic complaints such as their head feeling heavy and their heart beating too fast. What this causes is that people start thinking that the underlying cause of these problems must also be physical. This can lead to a possible under-diagnosis of mental health related problems.

Conclusion

The government must invest more funds and resources for better understanding and equal regulations for mental and physical issues. Moreover, there must be more awareness campaigns. There also has to be accessibility and affordability which can draw more people toward getting the proper help and tools at the early stages of their troubles.

4

The Present and Future Implications of the Downward Spiral

"Mental Health is like falling from the sky; if you don't parachute in time, you are done."

Emotions are a complex part of the human experience. They can be positive or negative. Positive emotions, such as happiness, joy, and love, can boost our mood and make us feel good. Negative emotions, such as sadness, anger, and fear, are associated with feeling down and make us feel bad.

Sometimes, we can get stuck in a loop of unpleasant emotions. It starts with a negative event or experience, which triggers a series of unpleasant emotions, such as sadness, anger, or fear. These emotions lead to negative thoughts and behaviors, which in turn reinforce the negative emotions. This cycle of unpleasant emotions, which I refer to as the 'emotional loop' can be very difficult to break. The emotional loop can continue for weeks, months, or even years if not addressed, and is a vicious cycle that can lead to depression, anxiety, and other mental health problems.

We may not have control over everything that happens to us, but we do have control over how we respond. There are things we can do to intervene early and break the cycle.

First, let's take a look at the five stages of the emotional loop:

Stage 1: Sadness or Loneliness - The Starting Point

When we experience changes in our life, it's normal to feel some discomfort. This can be triggered by life events, such as the loss of a loved one, major life changes, a sense of disconnection

Figure 7

from others, or even making changes to work on one's mental health. During this stage, it's common to experience a range of emotions, including profound sadness, grief, and a sense of emptiness. Physically, one may feel fatigue, heaviness in the chest, or a lack of energy. This marks the beginning of the cycle.

Stage 2: Early Symptoms of Dejection - A Call for Attention

In the second stage of the loop, we begin to notice the early symptoms of dejection. These symptoms serve as a call for attention, indicating that something deeper might be going on inside us. Emotionally, we may start to lose interest in activities we once enjoyed, leading to a sense of apathy or indifference. Sleep disturbances, such as insomnia or oversleeping, may become apparent, and concentration and focus can become challenging. Thoughts may be clouded with negativity or self-doubt, and a sense of hopelessness can creep in.

Stage 3: Reinforcement of Warning Signs - A Crucial Crossroad

If the early symptoms of dejection are ignored, they may progress to the third stage: reinforcement of warning signs. During this stage, negative emotions intensify, and self-destructive behavior may emerge. People might constantly anticipate the worst, doubt their abilities, or experience frequent bouts of sadness and despair. Social withdrawal and avoidance can become pronounced, making it challenging to connect with others. There may also be changes in appetite and sleep patterns, accompanied by a sense of exhaustion or chronic fatigue.

Stage 4: Hopelessness - Descending into Despair

If the warning signs are ignored, we enter the fourth stage: hopelessness. What this stage signifies is not the fact that the case becomes 'hopeless' but rather the perpetual emotional state of the person. At this point, mental health is significantly impacted, and a deep sense of despair takes hold. Emotionally, feelings of emptiness, worthlessness, and helplessness prevail, making it difficult to envision a brighter future. Negative thoughts may dominate every aspect of life, making it challenging to find any hope or positivity. Social isolation becomes more extreme, and the desire for connection diminishes. Individuals may engage in self-destructive behaviors, neglect self-care, or withdraw from their support networks.

Stage 5: Clinical Disorders - Depths of Desolation

When hopelessness goes untreated, the mental well-being loop reaches its final stage: clinical disorders. In this phase, an individual's mental well-being is profoundly affected, negatively impacting relationships, work, and physical health. Emotionally, there may be persistent feelings of sadness, despair, or extreme anxiety that disrupt daily functioning. Thoughts may be dominated by self-deprecating beliefs, intense worry, or intrusive thoughts. Physically, symptoms such as fatigue, changes in appetite, sleep disturbances, and psychosomatic symptoms may be prevalent. Behaviorally, individuals may struggle with maintaining relationships, experience difficulties at work or school, or engage in self-destructive behaviors. This is the stage where seeking clinical help becomes a necessity.

Conclusion

The emotional loop starts with a tiny trigger but has great repercussions. If not broken, it can continue for weeks, months, or in some cases even years, resulting in significant consequences across various aspects of life. Functional impairment, academic and professional setbacks, strained relationships, financial burden, and long-term consequences are among the potential impacts of delayed intervention.

It's essential to recognize the importance of seeking support and taking action early in these stages to positively impact our mental health. Opening up and sharing how you're feeling with trusted individuals like friends, family, or professionals can provide comfort and fresh perspectives. Therapy can help individuals develop coping strategies, challenge negative thoughts, and build resilience. Early intervention significantly reduces the risk of developing more severe emotional conditions, allowing for a greater chance of recovery and improved mental health.

5

Ending the Hush-Hush: Removing the Stigma

"Shedding stigma is the first step to a lighter mind."

Historical Roots of Mental Health Stigma

The stigma around mental health has a long and complex history that goes way back in time. In the past, people thought that mental disease was brought on by either supernatural forces or a person's moral failing. They'd go for exorcisms and religious rituals to get rid of the 'demons'. Individuals with mental illness faced harassment, discrimination, and marginalization. They were institutionalized and force sterilized. Then came the 18th and 19th centuries, when psychiatric institutions sprouted up. The idea was to provide care, but things got out of hand. These places became overcrowded, neglected, and more like fancy jails than healing centers.

Fast forward to the early 20th century, when psychiatry started flexing its scientific muscles. Finally, mental health conditions were being studied seriously. But guess what? Despite all the progress, people still had this lingering social stigma. Blame it on movies, books, and the media for painting individuals with mental illnesses as ticking time bombs, completely loony, or morally bankrupt. It only added fuel to the fire of negative stereotypes and fear.

Despite advancements in understanding and treating mental illness, stigma continues to exist. People with mental illness still face discrimination and marginalization.

The weight of silence can cause lasting harm. According to the National Mental Health Survey of India, conducted in 2015–2016, about 13.7% of the Indian population, which is approximately 150 million individuals, are in the need of active mental health interventions. When people don't seek help, their mental health issues can get worse and lead to more serious symptoms and crises. Some might turn to harmful ways of coping, like drugs or self-harm, while others might become isolated and disconnected from their loved ones, making their mental health even worse. Negative attitudes and beliefs about mental illness can cause a lot of harm, both to individuals and to society as a whole, and can make those subjected to them a victim of discrimination, rejection, or even violence.

Figure 8

Examples of these types of stigmas include being labeled 'pagal' (meaning crazy), which can further marginalize individuals and make them feel ashamed of their struggles. Another stigma is the perception that individuals with mental health issues are dramatic or attention-seeking, dismissing their experiences as exaggerated or insincere. Some people may believe that such issues are not real and just in one's head, undermining the validity of mental health challenges and discouraging individuals from seeking help. Incorrect knowledge and propagating wrong beliefs can also contribute to stigma, which perpetuates harmful stereotypes and misconceptions about mental illness.

In this way, the stigmas associated with mental health issues, such as labeling, misconceptions, and invalidation, contribute to a cycle of silence and further perpetuate harmful attitudes.

The Stigma Tax: Psychological Price We Pay

When mental health issues go untreated, they can result in a stressed and unhappy environment, lost productivity, higher healthcare costs, and in extreme cases, even suicide. According to the World Health Organization, depression alone causes about $1 trillion in lost productivity every year. Thus the cost of this stigma is really high, for both individuals and society.

The detrimental consequences are manifold: individuals who experience stigma often endure diminished self-worth, reduced opportunities, and social isolation, hindering their path to recovery. Moreover, societal consequences include decreased productivity, strained healthcare systems, and economic burdens. By perpetuating misconceptions and fear, stigma creates barriers to seeking help and perpetuates discrimination.

The only thing more exhausting than having a mental illness is pretending like you don't, in fear of raised eyebrows and whispered judgments. Moving forward, the first and foremost need is to let go of this stigma and talk about mental health with a more open mindset. Only when we start normalizing mental illnesses and talk about mental health in a positive light can we start to deal with the depths of the problem.

6

Structural and Financial Barriers in Mental Health

"Breaking through the mental wellness barriers is like finding a hidden treasure chest in a sea of challenges."

Mental health plays a crucial role in our overall well-being, yet numerous barriers often impede individuals from accessing the mental health solutions they require. These get intertwined with the stigma and further complicates any semblance of a solution. These barriers can manifest at individual, social, and structural levels, and addressing them is essential to ensure everyone has equal access to effective mental health care. By understanding and addressing these barriers, we can create a supportive environment that promotes mental well-being and enables individuals to seek the help they need.

Individual Barriers

Individual barriers refer to personal factors that hinder individuals from seeking mental health solutions.

Lack of awareness: Many individuals may not have sufficient knowledge about mental illness, its signs and symptoms, and seeking the right treatment. Lack of awareness can make it challenging for individuals to recognize when they are experiencing mental health issues and to know where to seek help.

Cost: The cost of mental health care can be a significant barrier for many individuals, especially those without insurance coverage or sufficient financial resources. People may not be able to afford mental health treatment, including therapy sessions and medication, since it can be pretty expensive. This financial barrier can prevent individuals from accessing the necessary care and support they need.

Fear of medication: Some individuals may have concerns about taking medication for mental health conditions. They may worry about potential side effects associated with taking medication, or the belief that relying on medication is a sign of weakness. These fears can prevent individuals from seeking pharmacological treatment even when it could be beneficial or necessary for their mental well-being.

Figure 9

Social Barriers

Social barriers encompass factors within society that hinder individuals' access to mental health solutions.

Lack of cultural competency: Cultural competence refers to the ability of mental health providers to understand and address the unique needs and experiences of individuals from different cultural backgrounds. When mental health professionals lack cultural competency, individuals may feel misunderstood or face challenges in effectively communicating their concerns. This can create barriers to receiving appropriate and effective treatment, as cultural factors and perspectives may not be adequately considered.

Lack of support: Support from family, friends, and the community plays a crucial role in promoting mental well-being and facilitating help-seeking behaviors. However, some individuals may lack a supportive network, which can exacerbate their mental health challenges. Without a supportive environment, individuals may feel isolated, discouraged, or unsupported in their journey towards seeking and maintaining mental health solutions.

Lack of mental health providers: In certain regions, there is a shortage of mental health providers, including psychiatrists, psychologists, and therapists. This scarcity makes it difficult for individuals to find timely and accessible mental health care. Long waiting lists and limited availability of mental health professionals can discourage people from seeking help or make it more challenging for them to access the care they need.

Structural Barriers

Structural barriers include barriers that manifest themself at a systemic level.

Discrimination: Discrimination against individuals with mental health problems can lead to marginalization and create significant barriers to seeking help. Stigma and prejudice associated with mental illness can discourage individuals from openly discussing their mental health concerns or reaching out for support. Discrimination can also manifest in various settings, such as the workplace or educational institutions, further impeding individuals' ability to access the necessary mental health solutions.

Lack of insurance coverage: Comprehensive insurance coverage for mental health care is essential for individuals to access necessary treatments and services. However, not all insurance plans offer sufficient coverage for mental health conditions. High co-pays, limited coverage for therapy sessions or medication, or lack of insurance altogether can prevent individuals from seeking the mental health care they need.

Lack of government funding: Insufficient funding allocated to mental health services can result in limited resources, understaffed facilities, and long waiting times for treatment. When mental health services are underfunded, it becomes challenging to meet the demand for care, resulting in reduced accessibility and quality of services. This can leave many individuals without adequate support and hinder their ability to access timely and effective mental health solutions.

Conclusion

Overcoming barriers to mental health solutions requires a multifaceted approach that addresses individual, social, and structural challenges. By educating the public, increasing access to providers, making mental health care affordable, and fostering support systems, we can dismantle these barriers and create a more inclusive mental health care landscape. Additionally, by advocating for policy changes, adequate funding, and combating discrimination, we can promote equal access to mental health solutions for all individuals. It is through these collective efforts that we can build a society that prioritizes mental well-being and ensures that nobody is left behind in their journey towards better mental health.

7

Pandemic Within the Pandemic: How COVID-19 Catalyzed Mental Health

"The pandemic's lasting toll on society's mental health is a concern that lingers long beyond COVID."

As the world grappled with the devastating effects of the COVID-19 pandemic, an unseen crisis emerged, silently ravaging the well-being of millions; what I call the mental health pandemic. In the wake of lockdowns, isolation, economic instability, and the fear of the unknown, individuals worldwide found themselves on the front lines of a battle against anxiety, stress, and despair.

After its emergence in 2019, COVID-19 rapidly turned into a devastating pandemic in 2020. Millions of people around the world lost their lives, and even more were infected or severely affected by the disease. While a large population recovered from the virus, it left a profound impact on the minds of many, resulting in ongoing struggles with mental health issues. There are a number of factors that contributed to the mental health crisis during COVID-19. These include:

The fear of contracting the virus: The COVID-19 virus caused a serious threat to health, and many people were understandably afraid of getting sick. This fear led to anxiety and stress.

The social isolation and economic hardship caused by the pandemic: The pandemic forced many people to isolate themselves from friends, family, and loved ones. This social isolation resulted in loneliness and feelings of despair. The economic hardship caused by the pandemic led to financial stress, which further contributed to mental health problems.

The disruption of daily life: The pandemic disrupted our daily lives in many ways. We had to adjust to working from home, homeschooling our children, and avoiding social gatherings. This disruption was undoubtedly stressful and overwhelming.

We can divide the course of the pandemic into three phases:

Initial Phase: This was the early stage in 2019 when the world was just beginning to learn about the COVID virus. Only a few individuals were infected during this time, and as a result, the impact on mental health was limited to a small number of people. There surely was some anxiety among people over what this virus was and what it meant, but the spread of information as well as the disease was relatively limited.

Middle Phase: In the beginning of 2020, the COVID-19 pandemic started spreading rapidly. Starting from China, it began to impact the entire world. Within the next two months, the number of infections increased significantly, and the death toll continued to rise. Almost all the countries imposed a lockdown which got extended from weeks to months. During this phase, the widespread transmission and increased fatalities had a profound impact on people's mental health. Even individuals who did not get the virus had their mental health compromised. These were individuals who either feared getting infected themselves or had a close one who was infected or had lost their life due to the disease. Additionally, the effects of the lockdown, such as social distancing, hand washing routines, the suspension of educational activities, witnessing friends and relatives struggling with the disease, and the overall atmosphere of worry and fear, contributed to the deterioration of people's mental health.

Final Phase: The current time represents the final phase of the COVID-19 pandemic. While there has been a decline in the number of individuals infected or succumbing to the virus, this disease continues to impact people's mental health. The trauma of losing loved ones, the stress of losing jobs and educational opportunities, the fear of contracting the virus, and all the other challenges that COVID-19 has brought upon millions of people, continue to significantly affect their mental well-being even today, and perhaps will continue to do so in the future. Moreover, COVID-19 has instilled a sense of uncertainty within individuals. Witnessing such a devastating disease and never having imagined experiencing such a situation has created a feeling of unpredictability. As a result, many people now harbor fear of COVID-19 or any other pandemic, which can manifest as anxiety and potentially lead to serious mental health conditions.

How is poor mental health taking the form of a pandemic like COVID-19?

The four factors of Climate, Conflict, Contagion, and Conformity are greatly impacting people's mental health, with COVID-19 having the most powerful effect. While the COVID-19 pandemic has receded now, issues related to poor mental health are rapidly

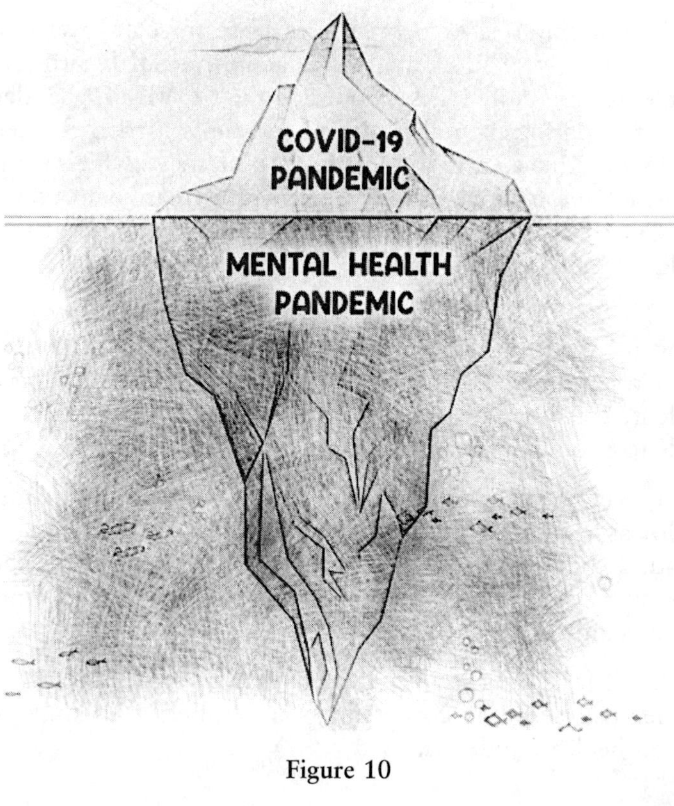

Figure 10

increasing. Just as millions of people have been affected by the disease, which is referred to as a pandemic, I think it would not be wrong to consider the deteriorating mental health of millions of individuals as a pandemic as well. Let me present some stats to explain.

According to research around happiness index in India, in 2011, approximately 89% of people were happy and living a good life. Just seven years later, in 2018, this figure declined, and only 66% of people considered themselves happy. By 2023, this number has further decreased, with the biggest reason being the COVID pandemic. Currently, in my view only 30 to 40% of people are leading a happy life, perhaps even lower. Covid would have had a similar impact across most parts of the world, driven by suffering of what has happened and the fear of what uncertain future may lie ahead.

Just as millions of people have been infected by COVID, today, millions of individuals are facing mental health-related problems on a daily basis. Alongside the COVID-19 pandemic, the deteriorating mental health of people is further worsening day by day due to a myriad of causes, many of which we have discussed in the above chapters. Just as the treatment of diseases like COVID is necessary, the solution and treatment of mental health-related issues is equally important.

The catch is, while most people display symptoms after being infected with the coronavirus, mental health issues are often not immediately visible, and by the time they become evident, considerable time passes. This delay in identification leads to problems becoming more serious.

Therefore, it would not be wrong to consider poor mental health as a pandemic. In my opinion, this pandemic is more dreadful than the COVID pandemic, as it has already spread extensively but remains largely invisible, and there is no clear end in sight.

In the following section, I will list solutions which, according to me, will serve as cornerstones in dealing with this global mental health pandemic.

Section III

SOLUTIONS

1

The Path to Mental Wellness: 5 Milestones

"Pack your emotional baggage, and welcome to the 'Transformation Vacation'."

Mental health is a complex and often difficult-to-understand subject, ranging from various emotions and thoughts to behaviors that keep shifting like quicksilver. One moment you think you've got it all figured out, and the next, it's like the universe hit the reset button! A mental health journey looks different for everyone, and it may involve recovering from a mental illness or navigating the path of managing and living with their mental health condition. When it pertains to our mental health, a quick fix is rarely possible. It's a journey, and like every adventure, it has its ups and downs. To make this journey easier to comprehend, I have divided it into five milestones, representing five stages.

These five milestones are as follows:

Milestone 1: Stigma - Breaking Free from Society's Chains

The journey begins with the formidable barrier of stigma. When individuals first encounter mental health challenges, they may find themselves hesitant to acknowledge their struggles due to the fear of judgment, ridicule, and shame. The haunting questions of "What will people think of me?" or "Will I become a subject of mockery?" lurk in their minds.

To overcome this stigma, it's essential to realize that mental health problems are as normal as any other health issue.

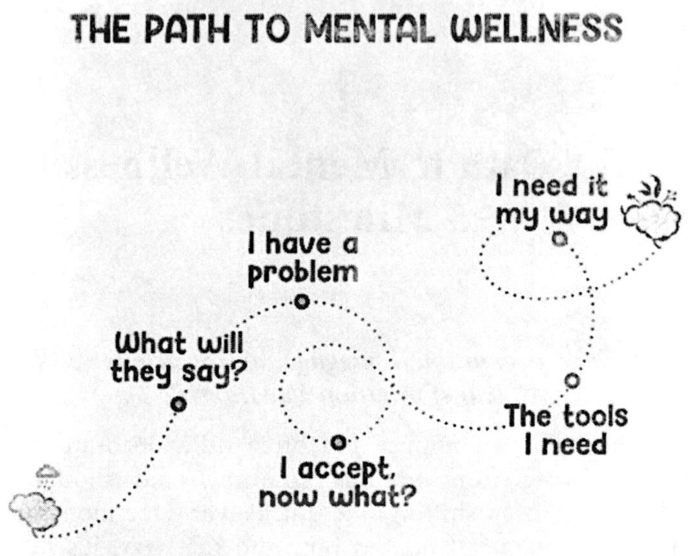

Figure 11

Acceptance of our challenges is the first step towards liberation. By understanding that people will always have something to say, we can gradually dismantle the stigma and set ourselves free to embark on the path of healing. We have already discussed how to achieve this previously in this book

Milestone 2: Acceptance - Embracing Our Inner Journey

Acceptance is the pivotal milestone where we courageously embrace our mental health issues without fear of societal judgment. This empowering step involves acknowledging the existence of our struggles and embracing them as an essential part of our being. Only by accepting our challenges can we truly seek the help and support we need.

While we are making progress in normalizing conversations around mental health, most people still struggle with acceptance for themselves. Everyone else is acceptable to some degree. As we accept ourselves, we liberate our minds from the weight of shame and are better equipped to explore the various facets of our mental health. This leads us to the next milestone: discovery.

Milestone 3: Discovery - Unraveling the Depths of Our Mental Landscape

With the chains of stigma broken and the burden of shame lifted, we can delve into the depths of our mental landscape. In this stage of discovery, we explore the intricacies of our emotions, thoughts, and behaviors. We identify patterns, triggers, and underlying issues that influence our mental well-being.

Embracing this journey of self-discovery, we gain insights into our strengths and vulnerabilities. Here comes the question, "I accept, now what?". Even the choice of whether they should go to a psychiatrist or a psychologist is filled with confusion. We will provide an easy-to-use cheat sheet for it further in this book. This newfound awareness paves the way for the next milestone: Tools and Solutions.

Milestone 4: Tools and Solutions - Equipping Ourselves for Healing

Armed with knowledge and understanding, we enter the milestone of Tools and Solutions. Here, we seek out various aids, treatments, and approaches that can help restore balance to our mental well-being. In my view, pharma-neuro intervention is much further in the search for solutions. That should be a curative approach when the chips are really down.

The first step to tools must be an individual using their vocabulary and acceptance of mental wellness to work on themselves. The best approach is to engage in what stimulates you. Next is using the power of community and people around you. Only then comes pharma-neuro intervention. For those with already worsened conditions, pharma-neuro can be the first step. Just as every individual is unique, so are the challenges they face on their mental health journey. The tools and solutions we choose are tailored to our specific needs and personality.

As we integrate these tools into our lives, we set the stage for the final milestone: Personalization.

Milestone 5: Personalization - Crafting Our Path to Mental Wellness

At the summit of our journey, we reach the milestone of Personalization. In this stage, we become the architects of our healing journey, carefully selecting the best combination of tools and solutions that resonate with our individual needs.

This deeply introspective process involves aligning our chosen approaches with our unique personality, preferences, and goals. We personalize our journey towards mental wellness, making it a tailored and holistic experience.

These five milestones encapsulate the journey from the deterioration of one's mental health to its restoration. Each milestone builds upon the previous one, propelling us forward on a journey of growth, resilience, and healing. To summarize, the five milestones include recognizing and accepting our problems after overcoming societal fears or shame to personalizing solutions for improving or restoring deteriorated mental states.

Remember, the road may be challenging, with twists and turns, but triumphs and newfound strength also mark it. By traversing these milestones with courage, compassion, and determination, we can navigate our mental health journey with greater understanding, leading to a life of balance and well-being. There is an additional sixth step that many use and is sometimes considered extremely therapeutic, that is to share their journey, learnings and experiences. Considering one of the key components of every individual's mental health is the mental health of its surroundings, this is self-preservation as much as it is altruistic.

2

The Power of Early Intervention

"It's always late, but never too late to work on your mental health."

In the realm of mental health, early intervention emerges as a powerful superhero, donning the cape of proactivity, equipped with strategies to address mental health concerns at their inception. This superhero's mission is to implement strategies and actions at the earliest possible stage to address mental health concerns before they escalate or become more severe, identifying and addressing risk factors, providing resources and support, and promoting mental well-being from the outset.

As you read in the earlier sections, it's crucial to act early when addressing a problem. The sooner we take action, the better the results tend to be. This early intervention not only helps us achieve better outcomes, but it also prevents negative impacts on the economy and other related factors. It's like catching a problem early and dealing with it quickly before it snowballs and worsens further.

Early intervention plays a crucial role in improving future outcomes for those affected. By intervening early, individuals can receive timely support and resources, reducing the severity and impact of mental health issues. This can lead to improved quality of life, prevention of chronicity, and positive effects on physical health. At the heart of early intervention lies a proactive strategy aimed at intercepting mental health concerns before they gain strength. It seeks to empower individuals by providing timely resources and support, fostering improved quality of life, and preventing the shackles of chronicity from taking hold.

Early intervention further extends to fortifying relationships and social connections, for they are the pillars upon which overall mental health rests.

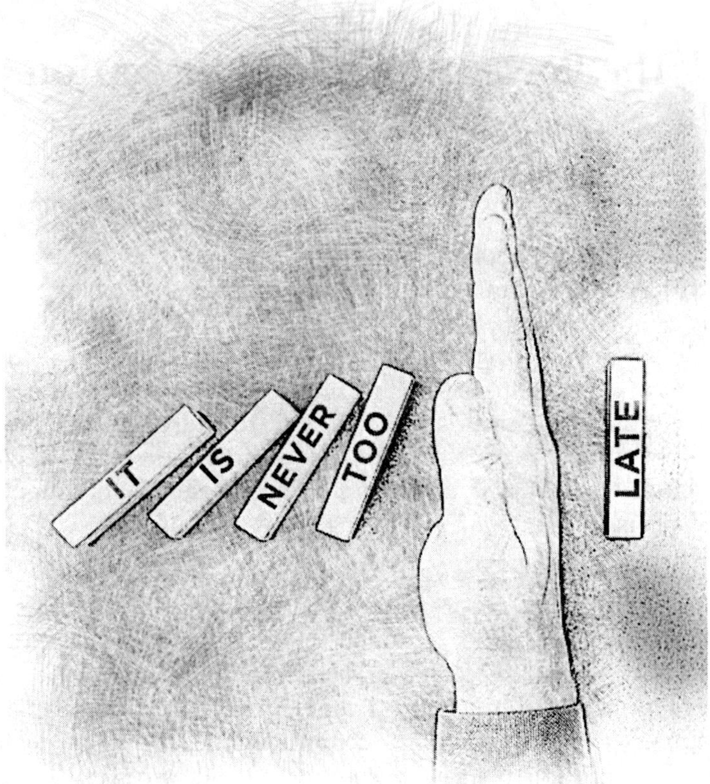

Figure 12

Across Age Groups, Settings and Culture

Early intervention strategies can be tailored to specific age groups and diverse settings to better address the unique needs of each of these groups. For children and adolescents, for example, it manifests in school and college-based programs that nurture mental well-being, impart essential coping skills, and instill the courage to seek help when needed. As it ventures into the realm of adulthood, it caters to the mental health needs of working professionals through workplace wellness programs and robust community-based support systems. For the elderly, it construes utilizing social engagement and health promotion programs to safeguard their mental well-being.

It is also important to consider cultural contexts when formulating prevention strategies. In a diverse nation like India, where cultural variations abound, interventions must consider factors such as cultural beliefs, practices, and social norms that play a significant role in shaping individuals' attitudes toward mental health and seeking help. Prevention strategies need to respect and incorporate diverse cultural perspectives to effectively promote mental well-being.

For example, I have heard people call depression a 'western concept', which might seem like an absurd statement to many, but remains something that many people in our country consider the reality. As a result, the way in which you deal with problems also starts differing. Some cultural contexts may require a focus on promoting social connectedness, while others may benefit from strategies that target reducing stigma associated with mental illness.

From Awareness To Action

Awareness acts as early intervention's trusted sidekick, heralding its arrival and alerting individuals to the presence of mental health concerns. However, awareness alone is not enough to defeat the forces of mental illness. Awareness is half the battle won, but it needs to be followed by action, encouraging individuals to recognize the signs and symptoms of mental health issues early on and empowering them with the tools to safeguard their well-being.

Early intervention also seeks to dismantle the barriers that hinder individuals from seeking help for their mental health concerns. Limited access to care due to financial constraints, stigma, or lack of resources can be significant roadblocks. To bridge this gap, promoting awareness and reducing stigma surrounding mental health is crucial. Furthermore, providing affordable and accessible mental health services can ensure that more individuals receive the timely support and treatment they need. It is through these actions that we can empower individuals to take charge of their mental well-being and seek assistance when required.

Crisis Intervention and Relapse Prevention

Another pivotal aspect of early intervention lies in its ability to avert mental health crises. Crisis intervention focuses on helping individuals regain emotional equilibrium during times of intense distress. This involves identifying risk factors and intervening proactively, so that professionals and support networks can provide timely assistance and support. This approach acts as a safety net, mitigating the potential harm or damage that could arise from untreated mental health issues. Crisis intervention training is necessary to equip professionals with the necessary skills to assess and de-escalate crises. Mobile apps, peer support programs, workplace intervention plans, and community collaborations are other ways to expand access to crisis support.

Strong emphasis also needs to be placed on supporting individuals throughout their recovery journey and improving their overall quality of life. Relapse, which is the recurrence of symptoms after a period of stability, can be mitigated by identifying triggers, developing coping skills, and building a support network. Factors such as stress, lack of coping skills, and substance use contribute to relapse, emphasizing the importance of planning and implementing strategies to prevent setbacks. Attending therapy sessions, taking prescribed medication, practicing self-care, avoiding high-risk situations, and being aware of personal triggers are effective ways to reduce the risk of relapse. By equipping individuals with coping skills, strategies, and tools to manage their symptoms, early intervention promotes long-term recovery and reduces the likelihood of relapses.

Transitioning from awareness to action is vital in the realm of mental health. Early intervention serves as a catalyst for positive change, enabling early detection, addressing underlying issues, improving access to care, preventing crises, and promoting recovery. By recognizing problems early and taking decisive action, individuals can receive the support they need, leading to improved outcomes and a higher quality of life. Through collective efforts, we can create a society that not only recognizes the importance of mental health but actively takes steps towards meaningful intervention and lasting change.

3

Thriving Basics: Eat, Sleep, Move, Breathe, Hydrate

"We ignore the basics because they sound too simple. But why can't the solutions be simple?"

In our pursuit of mental well-being, we often search for complex solutions and intricate strategies. We seek external remedies, therapies, and interventions, as they hold the key to unlocking lasting happiness and peace. However, in our relentless quest, we often overlook the power of simplicity - the profound impact that the basics of life can have on our mental health.

Embracing the basics means recognizing the fundamental elements that contribute to our mental well-being and integrating them into our daily lives. These essential pillars of self-care - eating, sleeping, moving, breathing, and hydrating - are not mere routine tasks to be checked off but vital practices that nourish our minds, bodies, and souls. They are the cornerstones upon which we can build resilience, foster growth, and create a solid foundation for mental well-being. Focus on the basics, and many problems will end automatically.

Eat Right: Nourish Your Mind and Body

The food we consume is more than mere sustenance for our physical bodies; it has a profound impact on our mental health as well. A balanced and nutritious diet can fuel our minds, enhance cognitive function, and stabilize our moods. By consciously choosing whole foods, incorporating fruits, vegetables, lean proteins, and healthy fats into our meals, we can experience heightened clarity, improved focus, and increased vitality.

Mindful eating practices such as savoring each bite, listening to our body's hunger and fullness cues, and cultivating a positive relationship with food can transform our eating habits into a source of nourishment and joy.

Sleep Right: Recharge and Restore

While we attempt to deal with the demands of life, sleep often takes a backseat. Yet, it is during sleep that our bodies and minds rejuvenate and recharge. Prioritizing quality sleep is essential for maintaining mental well-being. By establishing a consistent sleep routine, creating a calming bedtime ritual, and optimizing our sleep environment, we can enhance the quality and duration of our rest. When we prioritize sleep, we awaken with increased energy, sharper focus, and a greater capacity to navigate life's challenges with resilience.

Move: Harness the Power of Physical Activity

Physical activity is not only beneficial for our physical health but also plays a crucial role in supporting our mental well-being. This can be done through engaging in any kind of movement. Engaging in regular exercise releases endorphins, reduces stress, improves mood, and enhances cognitive function. Finding activities that we enjoy and incorporating movement into our daily lives can make exercise a source of pleasure rather than a chore. Whether it's dancing, hiking, practicing yoga, or simply taking a brisk walk, moving our bodies nurtures our mental health and empowers us to thrive.

Breathe: Cultivate Mindfulness and Inner Calm

We often forget the power of our breath. Mindful breathing practices, such as deep belly breaths, diaphragmatic breathing, or meditation, can help anchor us in the present moment, reduce anxiety, and promote mental clarity. By consciously connecting with our breath, we tap into a limitless source of tranquility, resilience, and self-awareness. Breathing mindfully reminds us to slow down, listen to our bodies, and cultivate a sense of inner balance amidst life's inevitable storms.

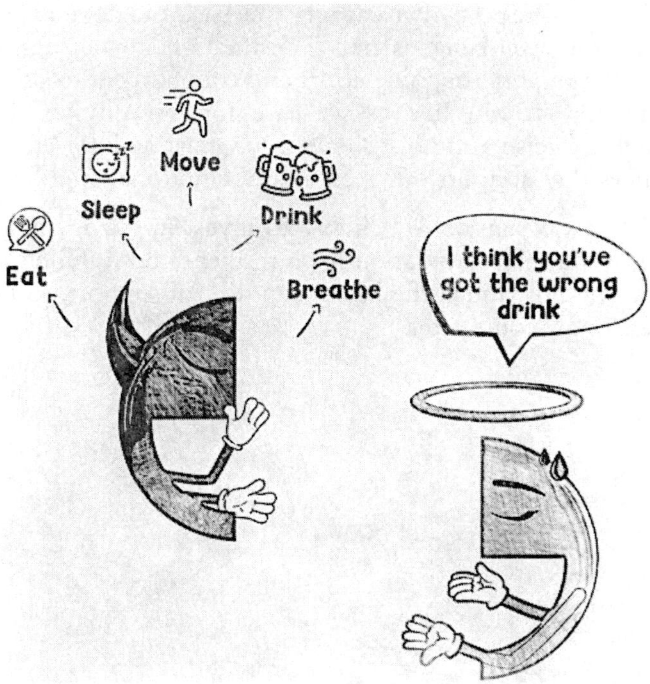

Figure 13

Hydrate: Quench Your Body and Mind

Water, the elixir of life, is essential for our physical and mental well-being. Staying hydrated optimizes brain function, improves mood, and enhances cognitive performance. By making a conscious effort to drink enough water throughout the day, we fuel our bodies and support our mental capacities. Hydration serves as a gentle reminder that even the simplest acts of self-care can have profound effects on our overall well-being.

In a world that often overwhelms us with complexities, returning to the basics offers us solace and a sense of grounding. By consciously focusing on our mental health and reflecting on our actions, we can break free from the cycle of reactivity and thrive on the basics. It is through this intentional approach that we can cultivate a deeper understanding of ourselves, our needs, and our triggers, leading to greater self-compassion and personal growth.

A crucial aspect of mastering the basics is acknowledging that mental well-being is not a destination but a continuous journey. It requires ongoing effort and commitment to prioritize our mental health. Just as we care for our physical bodies through exercise and nourishment, we must actively engage in practices that support our mental and emotional well-being.

When we consciously choose to invest in our mental well-being, we lay the foundation for a resilient and fulfilling life. It is amazing how much the basics can do. All support, tools and professionals come after.

4

The Healing Power of Words: The Connection Between Readership, Authorship, and Mental Health

"Outside of academics, 90% of authorship and 80% of readership involves mental wellness."

In the whirlwind of our modern lives, where stress and anxiety often feel like our constant companions, the quest for inner peace can seem like an unattainable mirage. Within the realm of literature, we discover an unexpected sanctuary of serenity and mental clarity. Outside of academics, 80% readership and 90% authorship is driven by mental health. Let's look at both of these one by one and delve deeper into this thought.

Reading: A Gateway to Inner Calm

Imagine this; you're nestled in your favorite reading nook, a steaming cup of your favorite beverage at your side, and an engrossing book in your hands. The mere act of diving into a different world, escaping the chaos of daily life, can be profoundly therapeutic.

Reading, in (almost) all its forms, is one of the most potent antidotes to the hustle and bustle of the modern world. It serves as a portal to far-off places, different eras, and the minds of countless characters. When you read, you invite fresh perspectives into your life, offering a respite from the ceaseless chatter of your own thoughts. Simply opening a book can remind you that there's a vast, beautiful world beyond your immediate concerns.

Consider the wisdom of mental health practitioners who often recommend reading as part of a holistic approach to well-being. They understand that in the midst of life's chaos, the act of reading can be a therapeutic escape—a moment to pause, breathe, and regain perspective.

Authoring: Unleashing Your Inner Wordsmith

Authorship is not merely about penning bestsellers; it's the art of writing itself, and it offers a treasure trove of therapeutic benefits waiting to be explored.

Writing, like reading, is an escape from the labyrinth of our own minds. It's a way to externalize thoughts, emotions, and experiences. Writing is the canvas upon which we paint our feelings, whether they're exuberant, melancholic, or somewhere in between.

Figure 14

It often occurs that people who are in a particularly challenging period in their life, turn to writing. Take the example of Anne Frank! It helps them externalize inner turmoil, giving voice to complex emotions and experiences. Writing became a trusted confidant, helping navigate the labyrinth of emotions and find inner peace.

The Harmonious Relationship Between Reading and Authorship

What makes this dynamic duo truly remarkable is their harmonious synergy. Reading exposes us to the wisdom and creativity of others, while authorship empowers us to engage in a dialogue with ourselves. Through reading, we learn to empathize with characters and their journeys, and through writing, we deepen our self-awareness.

Reading provides an escape, a chance to step into someone else's shoes, while authorship grants us a voice, an opportunity to articulate our thoughts and emotions. Mental health practitioners often recommend reading as a therapeutic practice, understanding its potential to offer solace and healing. It's a form of self-care, a retreat where one can find respite and rejuvenation.

In the words of Marcel Proust, "The real voyage of discovery consists not in seeking new landscapes, but in having new eyes". So, dear reader, whether you're lost in the pages of a beloved novel or pouring your thoughts onto the canvas of a blank page, know that you're on a journey toward inner peace. Embrace the therapeutic power of reading and authorship, and let them be your trusted companions on the path to a healthier mind.

5

Happiness, Peace, and Being Passionately Unattached

"Happiness is self-generated, not ambience acquired and certainly not situation dependent."

In the fast-paced rhythm of life, we tirelessly chase our dreams, relentlessly pursue success, all in the quest for that elusive state called happiness. Although everyone has different meanings and means for happiness, we all have this idea that when we get certain things in our life or only when specific dreams are fulfilled is when we will achieve 'happiness'.

We load our aspirations with expectations, convinced that only when we achieve them will we unlock the door to happiness. In this race of trying to reach the destination and achieve the supposed happiness, we become obsessed with our targets and carry massive expectations with them. We feel that if we aren't able to get the things we thought of, then we will be left with nothing, and we will be a failure.

Happiness is just one emotion among the many we experience daily. Humans experience a wide range of emotions in a single day - sadness, irritation, regret, joy, surprise, guilt, nervousness - these emotions are so fleeting in nature that expecting any of them to stay is akin to chasing an ever-elusive mirage. Amidst this relentless pursuit, we often overlook the most crucial ingredient for a fulfilling life: Peace of Mind. For me, peace is the most important ingredient to living a worthwhile life. To be happy, and be able to appreciate life, we need to have peace of mind.

Figure 15

Aligning Happiness and Peace of Mind

Lord Krishna wisely imparts in Chapter 2, Verse 47 of the Bhagavad Gita, "You have a right to perform your prescribed duties, but you are not entitled to the fruits of your actions." What he means by that is to pour your heart and soul into your endeavors, but don't do so for the purpose of seeking happiness from the outcomes. This leads to expectations which may not always be fulfilled. Instead, find happiness in the process - this will help you detach from the end result and, subsequently, find inner peace. While our aspirations may include lavish possessions and indulgences, it's essential not to overlook the simple joys that surround us daily. Happiness can also be found in the small things that aren't labeled as 'luxuries'.

When we look at happiness and peace of mind as two elements in the composition of life from this perspective, happiness becomes the 'passion' or the driving force which pushes us to perform our duties, while peace of mind becomes the feeling of being 'unattached' from the fruits of our actions. I call it being 'passionately unattached'.

This may appear paradoxical, but I have carried this ideology with me for most of my professional and personal life, and it is what has helped me keep my leadership as well as my mental health in check. Being passionately unattached means giving your all to everything you do while remaining steadfast even if it crumbles. This philosophy has been my ticket to success. I wholeheartedly commit to every aspect of my life, yet I wouldn't lose a moment's rest if any of it were to vanish overnight.

Why, you may ask? Because a passionately unattached lifestyle allows me to immerse myself entirely in my work. I can lead and perform my duties with genuine passion while maintaining the clarity required to address problems dispassionately. It's akin to a surgeon performing a heart surgery—precision demands detachment.

This approach permits me to enjoy the best of both worlds: genuine passion for achievement and the ability to remain unruffled, regardless of the circumstances.

I'm a fervent advocate for hard work and the exhilaration of a focused life. Nonetheless, I also recognize that genuine connections go beyond empathy and availability. To thrive in this world, one mustn't become overly attached to anything or anyone. For example, if my employees excel, I reward them warmly. However, if they choose to depart, I wouldn't flinch. That's the key to my happiness and effective leadership.

In conclusion, it's about passionately pursuing your goals while remaining unattached to the outcomes, finding delight in the journey, and preserving your mental well-being. That, dear readers, is the essence of being passionately unattached.

6

Holistic Healing: Complementary Therapies for Mental Well-being

"Therapy is a solution, not THE solution."

Prioritizing our mental health is crucial in the fast-paced, demanding world of today. While conventional methods like counseling and medication are essential for maintaining mental health, complementary therapies provide alternative ways to achieve harmony and peace in the body and mind. Professional-driven mental health services that are medicine-forward may not prove to be the most successful, particularly

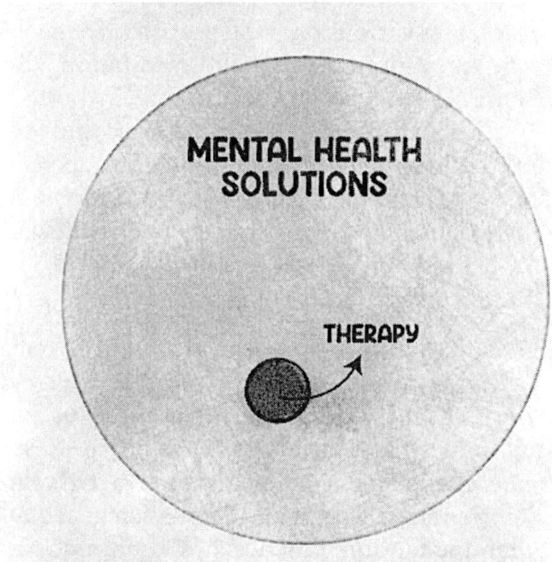

Figure 16

in eastern cultures. They are frequently founded on westernized conceptions of mental health and suffering, which leads to therapeutic approaches that are neither culturally appropriate nor practically adequate for (many) non-western situations.

This is where holistic medicine comes in - it is a form of healing that considers the whole person, which includes the body, mind, soul, and spirit. Instead of focusing only on the current symptoms of a mental health issue, it takes into account all mental and social aspects. It makes an effort to repair the complete body and deal with the underlying causes of problems with mental health.

In this chapter, I will introduce you to some popular complementary therapies: yoga, meditation, acupuncture, massage therapy, art therapy, and music therapy. The key belief is that people get mental health support by working in the area of their stimulation. You choose what stimulates you and get holistic support through that. Each of these therapies have their unique benefits and can contribute to improved mental health and overall well-being.

Yoga: Yoga integrates various physical postures (asanas), mindful breathing techniques (pranayama), and meditation (dhyana) to cultivate a sense of balance and tranquility in both the body and mind. By engaging in regular yoga practice, individuals can enhance their flexibility and strength while also experiencing a profound state of relaxation. Studies have demonstrated that consistent engagement in yoga can effectively alleviate stress, anxiety, and depression, thereby contributing to improved mental health and overall well-being.

Meditation: Meditation is a practice that involves focusing the mind and achieving a state of calm and clarity. By directing attention to the breath, a mantra, or an object of focus, meditation cultivates mindfulness and promotes inner peace. Research has highlighted the effectiveness of meditation in reducing stress, improving emotional well-being, and enhancing overall mental health. Regular meditation practice has been associated with increased self-awareness, improved concentration, and a greater sense of overall happiness.

Acupuncture: Acupuncture is a traditional Chinese medicine practice that involves the insertion of thin needles into specific points on the body. It is believed to improve the flow of energy (Qi) and restore balance in the body. Acupuncture has been reported to help alleviate various mental health concerns. While the scientific evidence supporting acupuncture's effectiveness for mental health is still evolving, many individuals find it to be a valuable adjunct therapy in their overall treatment plan.

Massage therapy: Massage therapy is a hands-on therapy that involves manipulating the body's soft tissues to promote relaxation and relieve muscle pain. It is commonly used to reduce stress and improve circulation. Massage therapy can also have a positive impact on mental health by promoting relaxation, and enhancing overall well-being. Research suggests that massage therapy may help decrease symptoms of depression and improve sleep quality.

Art therapy: Art therapy is a creative form of therapy that uses art to express emotions, explore thoughts, and foster self-discovery. Through various art techniques, individuals can engage in a nonverbal and symbolic communication process. Art therapy can be a valuable tool for individuals. It provides a safe and supportive environment for self-expression, promotes self-awareness, and facilitates emotional healing.

Music therapy: Music therapy is an evidence-based practice that utilizes music to address physical, emotional, cognitive, and social needs. Trained music therapists employ various techniques, such as listening to music, playing instruments, or creating music, to achieve therapeutic goals. Music therapy has been shown to reduce stress, improve mood, enhance communication skills, and boost self-esteem.

Dance, drawing/painting, dramatics, healing, pottery, spiritual beliefs and other activities are great sources of therapeutic support. Essentially, anything that moves you. Complementary approaches offer unique avenues for promoting mental health and well-being. These practices provide individuals with additional tools to manage stress, alleviate symptoms, and enhance overall emotional and psychological well-being. While these approaches may not replace traditional treatments, they can be integrated into a comprehensive care plan, providing individuals with a holistic approach to mental health. They can also help account for the cultural differences in mental health of individuals.

7

Spirituality and Religion: The Social Solutions for Mental Health

"Faith can be the ultimate antidote."

The fundamental objective of religion and spirituality is to give purpose and hope. These are two of the key ingredients of any mental wellness support system. Throughout human history, people have always searched for meaning and purpose in life. It's a deep longing that has guided individuals as they navigate the complexities of existence. Along the way, they have sought comfort and direction in the teachings and narratives found in spirituality and religion.

It's becoming widely acknowledged that spirituality and religion have a big influence on our mental well-being. When we talk about spirituality, we're referring to the personal and inner journey of finding meaning and purpose in life. Religion, on the other hand, involves organized belief systems and practices that are shared within communities. By examining the role of social support, coping mechanisms, and the cultivation of positive emotions, let me help you gain a comprehensive understanding of how spirituality and religion contribute to better mental health.

Social Elements of Religion and Spirituality

One of the key elements of spirituality and religion is the sense of belongingness that they bring with them. Being part of a religious or spiritual community provides people with a network of support, creating a vital foundation that allows them to maintain their mental well-being. These communities offer a safe space to connect with others who share similar values and beliefs, alleviating feelings of isolation and loneliness. Actively engaging in religious or spiritual practices and participating in community activities has been consistently associated with higher levels of social support. This implies those who are part of such communities perceive themselves as having more people they can lean on, which gives them a support system that can offer comfort, understanding, and guidance during challenging times.

Can Faith Help You Find Solace in Difficult Times?

Spirituality and religion provide individuals with a belief in a higher power or a greater purpose, which can be a source of comfort, hope, and meaning during difficult times. A belief in something beyond oneself can offer solace and a sense of perspective, helping individuals navigate and cope with stressors and providing a foundation of faith that supports them in finding inner strength and resilience. Religious rituals, such as prayer or meditation, serve as coping strategies that enable individuals to find solace and inner peace. Through rituals, they can cultivate a sense of calm, clarity, and renewed energy, enhancing their ability to cope with life's challenges and promoting mental resilience.

Positive emotions play a crucial role in mental health, and spirituality and religion offer numerous avenues for cultivating these emotions. Expressions of faith, such as singing, chanting, or dancing, can evoke feelings of joy, serenity, and transcendence. Engaging in acts of kindness, charity, and service to others, which are often integral to religious or spiritual practices, has been shown to enhance overall well-being and satisfaction with life. Additionally, the practice of mindfulness, commonly found in spiritual traditions, can promote self-awareness, reduce anxiety, and enhance emotional regulation.

Many religious and spiritual traditions offer a comprehensive ethical framework that guides individuals in their interactions with others. While they differ in many ways, both spirituality and religion share a core set of ethical principles that serve as a compass for leading a meaningful and virtuous life. These moral principles promote virtues such as compassion, empathy, forgiveness, and altruism, which are essential for healthy relationships and social connectedness. Living in accordance with these principles can lead to a greater sense of fulfillment, personal growth, and harmony with one's community.

Last few years have seen a tremendous growth in people turning to spirituality for seeking solace. This has also led to a significant increase in self-styled spiritual gurus, authors, self-help materials and various other alternate resources for people to get purpose and hope.

Conclusion

Spirituality and religion offer social solutions in the form of social support, belongingness and solace that can significantly contribute to mental health and well-being. By adhering to ethical guidelines offered by spirituality and religion, individuals can develop a strong moral compass that positively influences their mental well-being and their impact on society.

While religion and spirituality are something that not every individual follows or believes in, it becomes crucial to recognize and respect the fact that different individuals may find solace and meaning in various traditions. By embracing these dimensions of the human experience, we are led to the realization that it is all about what you believe in and what works well for you.

8

Developing and Recovering PsyCap: Get Your Mental Money Back

"Remember, setbacks are just the comma in the sentence of success – they don't stop the story."

Just as we can experience financial losses when investing money, our mental well-being can also suffer setbacks and downturns. We invest our mental energy in various areas of life, such as our careers, relationships, personal goals, and overcoming daily challenges.

However, sometimes these investments don't yield the positive results we hoped for, leaving us emotionally drained or overwhelmed. This results in a loss of psychological capital. We talked about this in the earlier chapter on Psycap—the harmful impact of this loss extends beyond ourselves and can affect the people around us. Our emotional state and psychological well-being influence our relationships, productivity, and overall demeanor. When we are emotionally drained or overwhelmed due to a loss, it can lead to increased stress, irritability, and a diminished capacity to support and engage with others effectively. Our relationships may suffer as a result, as our negative state of mind can strain interactions and hinder our ability to offer support and encouragement.

Psychological capital is important because it can help people cope with stress, bounce back from setbacks, and achieve their goals. When people lose psychological capital, they may find it more difficult to deal with challenges and may be more likely to experience negative emotions.

In the context of psychological capital, the journey of recovery involves acknowledging our past struggles and recognizing that perfection is not the goal. It's essential to understand that setbacks and losses are a natural part of life and they do not define our worth or potential for future success. Instead, the focus shifts towards utilizing the wisdom we've gained from our experiences to cultivate positive changes in our lives. In the process, we recognize our strengths and weaknesses and learn to trust in our ability to overcome challenges.

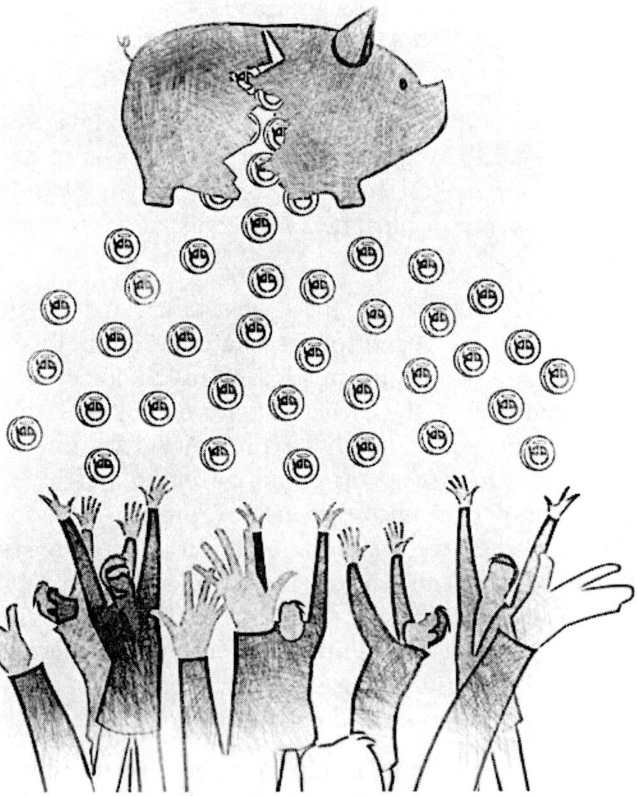

Figure 17

Reclaiming your well-being is a unique and personal journey. While there's no one-size-fits-all approach, there are strategies that can support the healing process. Surrounding yourself with supportive friends, family, or support groups can provide understanding, encouragement, and a sense of belonging. Sharing experiences with others who have faced similar challenges can be comforting and help alleviate feelings of isolation. Prioritizing self-care is crucial and can enhance emotional resilience and overall wellness. Breaking down your recovery journey into manageable steps and setting achievable goals is also important. Slowly working towards your goals and counting the little wins along the way is essential. At this time, mental health professionals, like therapists or counselors, can provide valuable guidance. Exploring alternate therapies like yoga, dance or art therapy can also prove to be beneficial.

Conclusion

Remember, you've the power to grow and transform from what you've been through. Your past doesn't have to define you or hold you back. It's about embracing the idea that we can use our experiences as stepping stones to a better future. This journey isn't one we have to tackle alone. We can lean on the support of our loved ones, seek guidance from therapists, or join support groups. Connecting with others who have faced similar challenges can provide us with comfort, encouragement, and fresh perspectives.

So, as we travel this road of PsyCap, let's keep in mind that it's not about striving for perfection or erasing our past struggles completely. Instead, it's about using the lessons we've learned to make positive changes in our lives, build resilience, and create a future filled with greater well-being and fulfillment.

9

Revolutionizing Mental Health: Harnessing the Power of Digital Technology

"Brace your neurons for a tech-tastic twist in mental well-being and Ctrl+Alt+Delete the stress."

In the past, seeking support was often difficult. People had to wait long periods of time to get help; they struggled to find qualified professionals, and they felt ashamed about asking for help. There were problems with accessibility, availability, affordability and acceptance. However, things are starting to change thanks to technology.

The answer to all questions of humanity (perhaps except salvation) in the 21st century lies somewhere in the realm of technology. It's creating a ubiquitous, pervasive, connected environment where access to anything and everything is possible.

Enter Digital Technology

We're in the midst of a digital revolution that's transforming how we take care of our mental well-being. It's making support more accessible and putting us in control of our own mental health. With all the advancements in technology and the way we stay connected, we now have exciting new ways to improve our mental well-being. It's a breath of fresh air, removing barriers and giving us the tools to heal and grow in ways that work for us.

There are now many online resources that offer support, such as chat rooms, forums, and websites. These resources can provide immediate and confidential support to people, without them having to worry about stigma or discrimination. Additionally, technology has made it easier to find qualified professionals. There are now many online directories that list mental health professionals, and people can easily search for a therapist who is a good fit for them.

Digital technology is revolutionizing mental health care. Smartphones, wearable devices, and online platforms are making it easier than ever for people to access mental health support. These technologies can help people identify and manage their mental health challenges, connect with others who understand what they are going through, and find the resources they need to get better.

Here are some of the ways that digital technology is changing the game for mental health:

Mental Health Apps: Nowadays, there are tons of apps designed to support our emotional well-being. These apps offer various tools and resources to help us manage our mental health. For example, they might have features to track mood, provide guided meditation exercises, or even offer virtual therapy sessions. These apps empower us to take an active role in looking after our mental well-being.

Online Support Communities: Thanks to digital platforms, we can now connect with others who are going through similar challenges. These online support communities give us a safe space to share our experiences, ask for advice, and feel like we have a community. It's a way to fight against the feeling of being alone that often comes with mental health struggles.

Teletherapy and E-Counseling: Digital technology has also allowed us to have therapy sessions from the comfort of our own homes, no matter where we are. We can connect with therapists remotely through video calls or online platforms. Studies have shown that remote therapy can be just as effective as in-person sessions.

Data-Driven Insights: Digital platforms collect and analyze data about mental health, and that can give us some really helpful information. Researchers can discover patterns, trends, and factors that contribute to mental health issues. This knowledge helps us understand these challenges better and find ways to prevent them. Plus, using data can lead to personalized treatment plans that are tailored to each individual's needs.

These are just a few examples of how digital technology is changing the way we approach mental wellness. It's making support more accessible, connecting us with others who understand, and giving us tools to manage our mental health better. It's an exciting time where technology is playing a vital role in improving our well-being.

Benefits

Digital technology has revolutionized mental health support in many ways. It has made it easier for people to access support from anywhere, at any time, and at a lower cost. Here are some benefits of using digital technology for mental health:

Accessibility: Digital mental health tools provide better access to support. This is particularly beneficial for people living in remote areas or with limited mobility who might have otherwise struggled to access mental health services.

Affordability: Digital mental health solutions, such as apps and online therapy platforms, often offer more affordable alternatives to traditional therapy sessions, making support more accessible to a wider range of individuals.

Convenience and Flexibility: Digital technology allows people to access mental health support at their convenience, without having to stick to strict appointment schedules. This flexibility accommodates busy lifestyles and enables people to seek support whenever they need it.

Personalization: Digital mental health tools can provide personalized interventions and resources tailored to an individual's specific needs, through data-driven insights and machine learning algorithms.

Anonymity and Reduced Stigma: Online platforms and apps offer individuals the opportunity to seek support anonymously, reducing the fear of judgment or stigma.

Self-Empowerment: Digital mental health tools empower individuals to take an active role in managing their mental well-being. Through mood tracking, self-help exercises, and educational resources, individuals gain a better understanding of their mental health and develop skills to cope with challenges more effectively.

Early Intervention and Prevention: Digital technology enables the identification of early warning signs and risk factors for mental health issues. By leveraging data analytics and machine learning, digital tools can help detect patterns and provide proactive interventions, potentially preventing the onset or escalation of mental health conditions.

Supportive Communities: Online support communities and peer-to-peer platforms foster connections and a sense of belonging among individuals facing similar challenges. These communities provide a space for sharing experiences, offering support, and reducing feelings of isolation.

Research and Advancements: Digital platforms generate a wealth of data that can contribute to advancements in mental health research. By analyzing this data, researchers can gain insights into the prevalence, causes, and effective interventions for mental health issues, leading to improved treatments and support strategies.

Conclusion

Digital technology is changing the way we take care of our mental well-being by giving us helpful tools and support. We can use our smartphones and devices to keep track of our mental health, connect with others who understand what we're going through, and even get professional help when we need it. It's exciting to see how technology is making mental wellness a priority and helping us understand and support it better.

As we move forward, it is important to consider the privacy, accessibility, and affordability of digital mental health tools. We need to make sure that everyone has access to these tools, regardless of their income or location. We also need to be mindful of the potential privacy risks associated with using digital technology for mental health purposes. Despite these challenges, digital technology has the potential to revolutionize the way we take care of our mental health. By embracing digital technology in the right way, we can create a future where mental wellness is valued and supported like never before.

I've spent my life advocating for the use of technology. I believe that it has the potential to improve our lives in many ways, including our mental health. Of course, any new technology is met with fear and distrust. When AI was first introduced, people were worried that it would replace humans. But as we've seen, AI is not a threat to humanity. Instead, it has the potential to be a powerful tool for good.

This is true for mental health as well. Technology has the potential to revolutionize mental health care. It can be used to provide access to care for people who live in remote areas, have disabilities, or who cannot afford traditional therapy. It can also be used to track symptoms, provide coping mechanisms, and connect people with support groups.

Having said that, mental health is one area where we need to be very careful in using technology. Technology is not a cure-all. For example, the race to create chatbots for everything - while that works in other areas, mental health is different. People usually struggle with giving words to their deep emotions and thoughts, how would a chatbot grasp the non-verbal, human aspect of these words? It cannot replace the human connection that is essential to mental health care. So the verdict in my view is to use technology, albeit carefully.

One such tool is Solh Wellness, a comprehensive mental health platform that I founded. Solh was founded with a core belief that mental health is a universal human right, which means it has to be available for everyone to use. Solh's mission is to make mental health support affordable, 24/7 accessible, available, personalized, and accepted across the world by providing an AI-driven non-judgmental safe space for people to express themselves and seek support to prevent clinically diagnosed mental disorders.

Mental health is just as important as physical health. Everyone deserves access to the resources they need to improve their mental well-being and realize this universal human right, which is why the platform is designed to be a personalized experience for each user, with a variety of free tools and solutions to meet their individual needs.

In the subsequent section, I will be talking exclusively about Solh. We will explore the platform in more detail and discuss how technology can help people achieve their mental wellness goals.

Section IV

SOLH

1
The Solh Way

"Mental health solutions must go beyond "when there is blood on the street, there is money to be made"."

As I delved deeper into the mental wellness space, three critical realizations compelled me to believe that there is an urgent need to take action. Firstly, it became evident that comprehensive efforts were required to combat the stigma surrounding mental health. There was a big need to address the social and cultural barriers that prevented many individuals from seeking help. 16-hour theory and the simplification of mental health into 5 easy adjectives seemed to be the perfect way to do it.

Secondly, while many startups were entering the mental wellness space, it became evident that most were solely focused on creating quick fixes. The urgency of the situation seemed to overshadow the importance of developing longer-term, sustainable solutions. I call this the second world war phenomenon of "when there is blood on the street, there is money to be made". It was apparent that for real change to occur, an investment of time, effort, and genuine commitment was crucial. The solution needed to not only address immediate needs, but also lay the foundation for lasting mental wellness. And some of this wasn't pure altruism, for me it even made business sense. In fact, I think this short-term focus is why none of the players in mental wellness became big, especially in India.

The third realization was perhaps the most profound – the lack of distinction between mental illnesses and everyday stress. It became apparent that many people struggled to differentiate between those experiencing extreme mental health issues and those dealing with the common stressors of everyday life.

Understanding this crucial distinction was vital to developing targeted interventions and support systems, because the everyday stress was the group which could potentially become the one with a mental illness. The need for preventive solutions in this context was evident.

In the wake of the COVID-19 pandemic, a pressing need for mental wellness solutions became evident. The world faced a crisis of deteriorating mental health, as the pandemic brought about significant changes in people's lives. From remote work arrangements to online schooling, individuals struggled to adapt to this new way of living. It was apparent that something had to be done urgently to address the growing mental health challenges that threatened to become a pandemic of its own. I could see this challenge everywhere, in every life. It didn't matter who you are, the 4Cs (climate, contagion, conflict, conformity) impacted everyone irrespective of wealth, status, region, gender, color, beliefs or any other structure. Everyone needed help.

With these convictions firmly in mind, Solh Wellness was born. Our vision was clear – to create a comprehensive and preventive mental health platform that would bridge the identified gap in the mental health ecosystem. Solh Wellness was not just about creating another app; it was about making a genuine impact on people's lives. We aim to provide 24/7 accessible, available, affordable, and personalized mental health tools and solutions to individuals and organizations alike, to make mental health accepted.

Recognizing the importance of mental health in workplaces, schools, and communities, we also extend our services to organizations through a subscription-based model, allowing us to offer our platform for free to individual users while reaching a broader audience and supporting various communities in their mental wellness journey.

At the heart of Solh Wellness lies a commitment to partnering with mental health professionals. By collaborating with psychologists, therapists, and counselors, we provide users with easier access to therapy. This strategic alliance not only

Figure 18

expands support for those in need but also empowers mental health providers to extend their reach and impact.

As Solh Wellness grows, so does our community of users. The positive impact of our platform has been evident through heartfelt testimonials and impact stories. Through this section, I invite you to join us on the journey of Solh Wellness – a journey that seeks to break down barriers, shatter stigmas, and foster a world where mental wellness is a priority for all.

2

A Personalized and Comprehensive Approach to Mental Health

"My mental health is my mental health; none of your mental health."

From the outset, Solh Wellness has attempted to recognize the barriers people face in accessing mental health support and created solutions in a way that effectively deals with these challenges.

While early intervention and preventive measures for mental health are crucial, they alone are not enough. In addition, approaches to mental health cannot be 'one-size-fits-all'. It is essential to provide personalized solutions that cater to the unique needs of every individual.

Through Solh Wellness, users gain access to a myriad of resources – from community support and counseling to mood tracking and other self-help tools – empowering them to take charge of their mental well-being. The app's AI-driven capabilities ensure that each user receives personalized recommendations tailored to their unique needs, fostering a supportive and empathetic environment. Our tools are designed to be universally accepted, affordable, 24/7 accessible, available and personalized to each individual's needs.

Our platform incorporates a comprehensive set of ever-evolving tools that can bridge the gap between mental health crises and their solutions, which has been categorized into three groups:

1. Self-Help Tools: These tools empower individuals to proactively take care of their mental well-being. Self-help tools need no one else, a person can use them as interaction with the platform. They include Self-Assessment, Goal Setting, Mood Analysis and Read and Learn.

2. Community Support: Recognizing the power of supportive environments, we designed community tools to foster a positive community for individuals needing mental health support. The key philosophy integrated within the platform is that of respect and privacy. There is always an option of anonymity built in the platform, which means you can share without fear and hesitation. With an added feature of My Diary, users have the power to control what they share and use the platform just for their own therapeutic writing. The community support features include Journaling, Solh Buddy, Support Groups and Anonymity.

3. Expert Services: While I have always maintained that preventive solutions are essential, there is absolutely a place for pharma-neuro intervention as well as other expert interventions in the form of therapy and other related services. This not only includes clinical interventions but also allied therapies. The tools in this category include Clinical Intervention, Allied Therapy, Packages and Subscriptions and Talk Now.

By incorporating these tools into your life, you can improve your mental health, leading to positive effects on overall well-being and a happier life. Our mission at Solh Wellness is to provide a comprehensive and inclusive platform for mental well-being, empowering individuals to take charge of their mental health journey with personalized and accessible support. Let's take an in depth look into these tools.

3

Tools and Solutions

"Democratizing mental wellness with personalized tools and solutions."

Self-Help

When it comes to mental health, taking care of yourself is not only important, but it also has lasting positive impacts. By proactively attending to our mental well-being, we can develop resilience, cope with stress more effectively, and foster a positive mindset, leading to increased happiness, improved relationships, and a stronger sense of self. Recognizing the urgent need to equip people with the necessary tools, solutions, and knowledge, we developed 4 powerful self-help tools on our platform. These tools are designed to empower individuals in coping with the challenges of daily life and building a resilient defense against mental health challenges.

Self-Assessment: Gaining Personal Insights

Self-assessments are a great way to figure out your strengths, your weaknesses and highlighting areas on which you can work on yourself. They can provide individuals with a structured framework to evaluate their mental health. For example, if you are having trouble sleeping and think it might be something serious, taking a quick test on insomnia can help you figure out if you need to get an expert opinion. Such tests are commonly referred to as Screening Tests.

To better understand oneself and identify areas of improvement, Solh provides a range of self-assessment tests.

These assessments cover various dimensions of mental health, including anxiety, stress, self-esteem, and more. By gaining personal insights through these tests, users can take targeted actions and seek appropriate support, creating a foundation for positive change and growth.

However, a necessary word of caution for using these tests - self assessments are not tools for clinical diagnosis. The main purpose of such tests is to support early detection and treatment. If your score on a particular test indicates a problem, you need to follow it by taking the expert opinion of a mental health professional. Only then can a clinical diagnosis take place.

For the future, we will keep exploring the use of AI as well as FER (Facial Emotional Recognition) for better reliability of these tests and for potential incorporation of a more measurable and objective approach to mental health.

Mood Analytics: Understand Your Emotions

Analyzing and recognizing patterns in our daily mood can provide valuable information about our emotional well-being. Recording your mood everyday can reveal insights about the impact of various factors, such as sleep, exercise, stressors, and social interactions, on our overall mood. This is a tool regularly employed by mental health professionals - they ask their patients to track their moods so that they can be in tune with how they are feeling and understand why they felt the way they felt.

Solh's Mood Analytics feature enables users to monitor and analyze their moods using a range of expressive emojis, including the Mann and Demann emojis. This self-awareness tool helps individuals identify triggers, patterns, and make necessary adjustments for a balanced and emotionally healthy lifestyle. This data can also serve as a valuable tool for clinicians in assessing the effectiveness of treatments, identifying potential triggers, and monitoring progress over time.

Looking at this history can be especially interesting. It can give us useful insights into our relationships or help remove the mask or preconceived notions about certain activities, elements or people that one may have.

Read and Learn: Educate Yourself

Learning is the most impactful way towards better mental health. The lack of awareness and knowledge is the core reason that we are struggling to deal with the problems of mental health. If people are made aware about the topic of mental health, less people would be afraid about coming out and asking for help.

Solh's Read and Learn section offers a wealth of informative content and blogs related to mental health and awareness. By educating users on various topics, this feature aims to broaden understanding, debunk misconceptions, and empower individuals to make informed decisions about their mental well-being.

Goal Setting: Charting a Path to Success

There are people who just can't function without a goal. It's a part of their psyche, their drive. Setting goals for them is the most important starting point, without which there can't be a start. A goal or an objective can be as small as waking up at a fixed time or as ambitious as hitting the gym 6 times a week. Our brains are wired in a way that produces a reward chemical called dopamine that makes us feel good when we reach milestones.

Solh empowers individuals to set meaningful goals and work towards achieving them. Whether it's personal growth, career aspirations, or general well-being, users can choose from a variety of predefined goals or create custom goals tailored to their specific needs. Through our platform, we provide a goal-setting feature that enables individuals to track their progress and move closer to achieving their desired outcomes. By regularly monitoring their progress, individuals can stay motivated, build resilience, and overcome obstacles.

Community Support

The power of our surroundings is undeniable when it comes to our mental health. The environment we find ourselves in plays a significant role in shaping our well-being. A positive and supportive community can make a world of difference in helping individuals navigate the challenges of mental health. That's why, at Solh Wellness, we have dedicated four tools to our community support category. These tools are designed to address feelings of isolation and provide the necessary knowledge and support to tackle mental health issues on a larger scale.

Journaling: Unleashing Personal Expression

Writing is a powerful tool which helps individuals in expressing themselves vividly. The Journaling feature was created around this idea - to allow people to write and express themselves, kind of like the Instagram of mental health. However, we differentiate ourself from social media platforms. While people on social media platforms try to portray a life that they don't have, we ensure that conversations on our app are genuine and committed to talking about mental wellness. Through this, the journaling feature transforms into a powerful outlet for processing emotions, reducing stress, and gaining insights into personal experiences.

Support Groups: The Power of Community

Having a group of people who understand you can be really comforting. It serves as a reminder that you are not alone, and provides an environment of acceptance and empathy. Support Groups are the perfect example of how the power of community can play a crucial role in providing understanding for individuals facing similar experiences and challenges.

Sometimes just knowing that we are not alone is therapeutic enough. At Solh Wellness, we recognize the importance of support groups in promoting mental well-being, which is why we have created a space that offers easy and accessible ways for individuals to join these valuable communities. Our user-friendly interface allows individuals to easily explore the available support groups and choose the ones that align with their interests and experiences. We also ensure privacy and confidentiality, creating a safe space where individuals can freely express themselves.

Figure 19

One key aspect of community support tools has to be the ability to get support in the language of one's own comfort. Converting your innermost feelings or challenges to words, then converting them into English or any other language on the fly - it can lose the context that it was originally meant in. Hence, Solh app has been carefully created in multiple languages. This means one can journal and participate in support groups and take therapies, all in their language.

Anonymity: Ensuring Confidentiality and Privacy

While we know that generating open conversations around mental health is important, anonymity is an extremely critical need for openness. For us anonymity is essential. Our mental health is a combination of the good, bad and ugly thoughts; all the shareable and unshareable aspects of our personality. There is always the fear of being judged, of the information one shares being misused.

Acknowledging this sensitive nature of mental health discussions, Solh App ensures complete anonymity for its users.

With the option to journal anonymously within groups and chat with counselors, individuals can freely express themselves without fear of judgment. This feature encourages open and honest communication, facilitating a safe environment for growth and healing. Anonymity also promotes a culture of understanding and empathy within our community. When individuals share their stories without revealing their identities, it levels the playing field and eliminates preconceived notions or biases. This allows others to focus solely on the shared experiences and provide support and guidance based on genuine empathy.

Solh Buddy: Your Mental Health Companion

Navigating the challenges of mental health can often feel overwhelming and isolating. Individuals may struggle to find someone who truly understands their experiences and can provide the support they need. In such times, a few words of encouragement are often enough to remind people that they are not alone.

Solh Buddy is an invaluable tool on our platform, designed to provide individuals with a supportive and understanding connection as they embark on their journey to mental wellness. The Solh Buddy feature acts as a trusted companion, offering insightful advice to individuals facing challenges. It assists users in journaling their thoughts and emotions, suggesting when it might be beneficial to consult a professional. By providing guidance and support, Solh Buddy ensures that individuals feel heard and empowered to take the necessary steps towards healing.

Expert Services

Addressing the challenges of mental health requires a careful and proactive approach. Seeking guidance from experts in the field is crucial in order to make progress towards better mental health. Our Expert Services category focuses on providing timely and accessible assistance from mental health experts.

Clinical Intervention: Expert Support at Your Fingertips

The right support at the right time can make a world of difference for someone navigating their mental health. We believe that accessibility plays a vital role in connecting individuals with the best experts suited to address their specific mental health concerns.

Solh's Professional Services encompass qualified mental health professionals, including psychiatrists, clinical psychologists, and counselors. These professionals cater to the specific needs of individuals, providing personalized care and evidence-based interventions. Our user-friendly platform gives users the option to search 'by issue' as well as 'by profession', allowing them to quickly find relevant resources and experts available on our platform. We believe that everyone deserves timely and appropriate help, and our platform is designed to ensure that individuals can find the best experts to guide them on their path to mental wellness.

Allied Therapy: Holistic Approaches for Well-rounded Healing

Mental health is a deeply personal and individual experience. Different individuals may respond differently to various therapeutic approaches. With this understanding at the core of our philosophy, Solh Wellness offers a range of allied therapies such as yoga and art therapy. These alternative therapeutic approaches complement traditional methods, empowering individuals to find healing and personal transformation through diverse modalities. Our goal is to offer a range of options so that each person can find the approach that resonates with them.

Creative therapies like Art, Music and Dance therapy, for example, provide a creative outlet for individuals to express themselves, process emotions, and explore their inner world through various artistic mediums. By offering these diverse therapeutic options and more, we aim to empower individuals to choose the therapy that aligns with their personal preferences, needs, and goals. We believe that everyone deserves access to help that resonates with them and supports their mental well-being journey.

Packages and Subscriptions: Affordable Mental Healthcare

There is no beating around the bush - mental health services are expensive! This is a common concern that often prevents individuals from seeking the professional support they need.

We recognise the significance of mental health care for populations such as students who may not be financially self-sufficient. To address this, we have taken great care in building our platform and therapeutic solutions to be cost-effective without sacrificing quality or effectiveness. We accomplish this in part by providing bundled packages that offer discounts. This allows people to seek help without cost being a barrier in their healing journey.

Talk Now: Immediate Support

I'm sure we all have faced a sudden feeling of being overwhelmed by emotions. What you often desire at such a time is someone who can listen to you. In times of emergencies or crisis, having versus not having a listening ear may end up having great repercussions.

Figure 20

With this realization, our Talk Now feature provides individuals with real-time access to in-house counselors, who are available 24/7. Whether in times of crisis, uncertainty, or simply when someone needs a listening ear, this on-demand service ensures that professional help is just a click away, offering comfort, guidance, and reassurance whenever it is needed most.

One of the key aspects of the Talk Now feature is that it is available at no cost. We believe that mental health support should be available to all individuals, regardless of their financial circumstances. By providing this service free of charge, we aim to eliminate any barriers that may prevent people from seeking help.

You are not alone in your journey towards better mental health. Reach out, talk, and let us be there for you. Together, we can overcome the obstacles and work towards a happier and more fulfilling life.

4

Mental Health is a Universal Human Right

"The powerhouse of human existence."

In a world where diversity is celebrated and human rights are championed, it's high time we recognized a fundamental truth: mental health is a universal human right. This realization has been a cornerstone of my advocacy journey over the past two years, and it's a sentiment that has even been echoed in the theme for World Mental Health Day 2023.

Mental health issues affect people from all walks of life, irrespective of their financial situation or level of education. To emphasize the urgency of addressing mental health on a global scale, consider the following statistics:

- One in four people will be affected by a mental health condition throughout their lifetime.
- One in eight people globally is living with a mental health condition.

These numbers make one thing crystal clear; mental health is not a niche concern. These issues don't discriminate based on race, age, gender, or geography.

Many people still believe that mental health related problems are only applicable to a small population of people. Let me give you an example - I bet you've heard someone say that mental wellness is just for the rich. We think that mental wellness is a problem for those who can afford it. We assume that only the wealthy can take the time to care for their mental health, with access to therapists and fancy retreats. But in reality, it's not about being rich; it's about having the means to access these resources. And that's where the divide begins.

Mental wellness isn't a luxury; it's a basic human right that should be accessible to everyone, no matter where you come from or how deep your pockets are.

It is a common misconception that only the affluent can afford the luxury of addressing their mental health needs. This perpetuates stigma and prevents those who are struggling from seeking the help they deserve. You see, mental health issues don't discriminate. They don't care if you're a CEO or an employee, an engineer, an artist, or even a mental health professional for that matter. Stress, anxiety, and depression can affect anyone, regardless of their socioeconomic status. In fact, those facing financial hardship often deal with extra stressors like unemployment, housing instability, and discrimination, which can take a toll on their mental well-being.

Mental health is also not a problem that limits itself to any geographical borders. It knows no borders. It can crop up in the bustling streets of New York City or in the serene countryside of rural India. It's not something which only affects the elite, and it is definitely not a 'western' concept.

The Five Pillars of Mental Health as a Universal Right

Affordability: Mental health care should be affordable for all, regardless of their financial situation. No one should be denied help because they can't afford it.

Accessibility: Mental health services must be readily accessible, geographically and logistically, to everyone. This includes rural communities, marginalized populations, and individuals with disabilities.

Availability: There should be an abundance of mental health services to meet the diverse needs of our global population. This means a variety of treatment options, from traditional therapy to alternative methods.

Acceptance (and Removal of Stigma): Society must recognize mental health conditions as legitimate illnesses and remove the stigma attached to them. Mental health issues should be discussed openly, like any other health concern.

Personalization: Mental health care should be tailored to the individual. No two people are the same, and their treatment plans should reflect that diversity.

Figure 21

A world where mental health is for everyone

Close your eyes for a moment and imagine a world where we treat mental wellness as an inalienable human right, just like access to clean water, food, or education - not as a luxury, but as a basic necessity. When we prioritize mental health as a right for all, we're not just doing something morally right, we're investing in the collective strength and resilience of our society.

Governments can enact policies and programs that shatter the barriers to mental health care. This means making mental health services affordable and accessible to everyone, regardless of their bank balance. Telehealth services, community clinics, and outreach programs are all part of the grand plan to ensure everyone can access the care they need.

But it's not just about the policies; it's also about education. When we teach people from a young age about mental wellness, we're not only reducing stigma, but we're also empowering them to take control of their own mental well-being.

In conclusion, mental wellness is not a luxury reserved for the elite; it's the birthright of every individual on this planet. By recognizing this, we're not just making the world a healthier place; we're making it a fairer and more compassionate one. So let's champion mental wellness for all and write a brighter, more inclusive future together.

5

Sustainability: Embracing Mental Wellness as a Way of Life

"Rome & mental wellness can't be built in a day"

In the bustling world of modernity, where the pursuit of success, advancement, and prosperity reigns supreme, the significance of mental health often takes a back seat. However, beneath the surface of material achievements lies the undeniable truth that mental well-being is the bedrock upon which a better and happier life is built. To truly flourish, it is essential to embrace the concept of sustainable mental health. But first, it is necessary to understand what sustainable mental health means.

Sustainable mental health is more than a momentary state of happiness; it is the equilibrium of one's mental well-being, nurtured and preserved through conscious efforts and time. Sustainable mental health, thus, refers to the stability of one's mental well-being over time. This can only be brought about through continued efforts to improve it and maintain it. Bringing stability to mental well-being ensures better mental health for both the present and the future, helping us keep it balanced in the long run. With sustained mental health, a person can not only be happier, healthier and more productive, but also improve their present and future with its positive effects.

Just as the world endeavors to achieve sustainable development and preserve the environment, there is also a need to make mental health sustainable in today's world. As various organizations tirelessly work towards sustainable goals, such as clean water, poverty eradication, and environmental conservation, it is high time that 'sustainable mental health' takes center stage in our collective consciousness. Unfortunately, despite its undeniable importance, mental health often remains neglected or even stigmatized, leading to severe consequences for individuals and society as a whole.

Figure 22

Why is the sustainability of mental health important?

Having a balanced mental health is important. The stability of mental health has positive impacts on the five adjectives that you have already read about, and it can contribute to improving both the present and future of an individual. Improved mental health enhances productivity, attention, physical health, and helps eliminate issues such as poverty, illness, and illiteracy, while promoting peace of mind, personal development, and overall well-being.

Mental health affects all these issues, and these issues are essentially the concerns or goals of development and environmental sustainability. This means that in today's era, the stability of mental health is of utmost importance.

What can be done for the sustainability of mental health?

To achieve sustainability in mental health, continued efforts are essential. Taking the smallest of steps towards a better mental health can eventually result in big rewards. By enhancing our psychological capital, that is an individual's positive psychological resources, such as optimism, resilience, self-efficacy, and hope, we can improve our mental health and contribute to its stability. Any activity that improves mental health or brings stability to it is associated with the five adjectives. Therefore, I believe that by working on the five adjectives daily, mental health can be provided with stability.

The Path Towards a Better Tomorrow

True prosperity lies not just in material wealth but also in the richness of mental well-being. By acknowledging the importance of mental health and dedicating ourselves to the pursuit of sustainable mental well-being, we pave the way for a brighter and more harmonious future.

Let us embark on the path of Solh – the journey towards happiness and peace of mind. Embrace the power within, nurture the seeds of resilience, and sow the dreams of a happier and healthier tomorrow through the sustained care of your mental health.

Section V

SDGs & MENTAL WELLNESS

I jokingly ask people, assuming you are successful in all SDGs and you create a perfect climate and world, yet people are still struggling with their mental health, in such a scenario have you really achieved anything? While sometimes I ask as a joke, this is a practical true question in my view. It puts mental health beyond everything else, beyond the SDGs, sometimes even beyond the pursuit of luxury, technology or basic necessities.

In my journey of exploring different mental health issues and their potential solutions, I can't help but recognize the connection between Sustainable Development Goals (SDGs) and mental health. The Sustainable Development Goals (SDGs) are a comprehensive set of 17 global objectives established by the United Nations in 2015. These goals serve as a universal call to action to address various critical challenges and promote sustainable development worldwide. While only the third SDG contains a direct mention of mental wellbeing, in totality eight of them - SDG 1, SDG 3, SDG 4, SDG 5, SDG 8, SDG 10, SDG 11, and SDG 13 - incorporate challenges that affect mental well-being worldwide.

Since independence, we have grown a lot as a country when it comes to development of cities, environment, equality, and education. It's been 75 years since India's independence and along the way, we have made giant strides. But is any of it worth it if we are struggling to be happy? This goes to show how important mental wellness is in development - this makes including mental health in the SDGs extremely necessary.

Mental health plays an integral part in the overall health of people, as is what we have discussed in this book, and thus it has a vital role in different SDGs as well. I will talk about these five different SDGs and how Solh Wellness can be a powerful platform in order to tackle such challenges, making the world better for everyone and helping further the vision of the SDGs.

1

Mental Wellness & SDG 1: No Poverty

SDG 1 aims to eradicate poverty in all its forms and dimensions, recognizing that poverty is not just about the lack of financial resources but also about the deprivation of basic human rights and access to essential services. Mental health plays a significant role in SDG 1, as poverty and mental health are intertwined in a complex cycle. Poverty can lead to mental health challenges, and conversely, mental health issues can perpetuate poverty, creating a vicious cycle that hinders individuals from breaking free from deprivation. In this chapter, I explore the profound connection between SDG 1 (No Poverty) and mental health, with a specific focus on target 1.4.

Figure 23

Correlation of Mental Health, SDG 1 Targets, and Solh Wellness

Target 1.4: By 2030, build the resilience of the poor and those in vulnerable situations and reduce their exposure and vulnerability to climate-related extreme events and other economic, social and environmental shocks and disasters:

This target seeks to ensure equal rights and access to economic resources and basic services for all, including the poor and vulnerable. However, mental health challenges can be significant barriers to accessing these, further exacerbating poverty and vulnerability among affected individuals. Solh Wellness aims to empower individuals to make informed decisions about their lives and resources by improving their mental health, promoting resilience and allowing them to bounce back from adversity.

Conclusion

SDG 1 and mental health are intricately linked, with mental health challenges often exacerbating poverty and vulnerability. Solh Wellness has been an invaluable resource in addressing mental health issues among individuals experiencing poverty and advancing the benefits of SDG 1 Target 1.4. We contribute to breaking the poverty-mental health cycle and promoting greater well-being and empowerment among vulnerable populations through accessible and affordable mental health support, breaking the stigma surrounding mental health, empowering decision-making, and offering holistic support. Together, we can create a future where mental health support is accessible to all, and individuals are empowered to break free from poverty and vulnerability, paving the way for a more equitable and inclusive society.

2

Mental Wellness & SDG 3: Good Health & Well-Being

Within the realm of the Sustainable Development Goals (SDGs), SDG 3 (Good Health and Well-being) plays a crucial role in addressing mental health as an integral component of overall health. SDG 3 addresses various aspects of health, focusing on physical, mental, and emotional well-being. Mental health is an important component of overall well-being and is recognized as a fundamental aspect of SDG 3. Addressing all the challenges related to mental health is essential for achieving the objective of ensuring healthy lives and promoting welfare for all. In this chapter, I delve into some important SDG 3 Targets: Target 3.4, Target 3.5, Target 3.8, and Target 3.d, which have important implications for mental health.

Correlation of Mental Health, SDG 3 Targets, and Solh Wellness

Target 3.4: By 2030, reduce by one-third premature mortality from non-communicable diseases (NCDs) through prevention and treatment and promote mental health and well-being

Mental health plays a significant role in reducing premature mortality from NCDs such as cardiovascular diseases, cancer and diabetes, which refers to the unconditional probability of death between ages 30 and 70 years. Premature mortality can be exacerbated by poor mental health, but it is currently excluded from global health initiatives. Solh Wellness promotes wellness of people by providing them with affordable and accessible resources, mental health tools & solutions, and empowering conversations to foster healthy lifestyle changes.

Target 3.5: Strengthen the prevention and treatment of substance abuse, including narcotic drug abuse and harmful use of alcohol

Mental health challenges, such as depression and anxiety, can contribute to higher rates of substance abuse. Prevention and treatment efforts can be enhanced by addressing various mental health challenges associated with substance abuse, breaking the cycle of addiction and improving overall well-being. Solh Wellness has taken a pledge to work on this by raising awareness and handling substance abuse, addiction, and mental health issues. We help individuals by providing them counseling, support groups, and educational campaigns.

Target 3.8: Achieve universal health coverage, including financial risk protection, access to quality essential health-care services, and access to safe, effective, quality, and affordable essential medicines and vaccines for all

Mental health is just as vital for human welfare as physical health. Therefore, all the costs related to it must be covered in the health insurance. A welcome step in this direction has been the inclusion of mental health in health insurance, as directed to insurance companies by the Mental Healthcare Act of 2017. Ensuring access to and availability of comprehensive and quality mental health care and essential medicines should be at the forefront of all efforts. Solh Wellness recognises mental health as a universal human right, and offers access to mental health resources to its users while providing many tools for free. Our mission is to connect users to quality care and mental health is one of the integral parts of comprehensive health care.

Target 3.d: Strengthen the capacity of all countries, in particular developing countries, for early warning, risk reduction and management of national and global health risks

By prioritizing mental health and seeking appropriate support and care, individuals can be better equipped to manage health risks and address health challenges promptly. Solh Wellness is committed to building mental health capacities in developing countries, where access to mental health resources may be limited. By offering localized content, culturally sensitive support, and multi-language features, we ensure that individuals in these regions can access the mental health support they need.

Conclusion

The intricate relationship between SDG 3 and mental health underscores the need to prioritize mental well-being in the pursuit of global health and well-being for all. Solh Wellness serves as a powerful tool in this regard. By contributing to a healthier and more resilient global community through generating mental health awareness, equipping people with the necessary tools and solutions required in this regard, providing access to quality care, and empowering them to prioritize their mental well-being, we are taking a step closer to achieving SDG 3 targets and building a future where everyone can live healthy, fulfilling lives.

3

Mental Wellness & SDG 4: Quality Education

Quality Education, i.e, SDG 4 is an important aspect to consider when we talk about shaping the future of individuals and societies, as it focuses on ensuring inclusive and equitable quality education for all. It aims to provide individuals with the knowledge, skills, and competencies needed for personal and professional success.

Mental health plays a vital role in achieving this goal, as individuals with good mental well-being are better able to engage in learning, cope with challenges, and develop the necessary social and emotional skills to thrive in educational settings. In my opinion, a conducive environment for learning, personal growth, and holistic development can be achieved through aligning educational initiatives with mental health support. In this chapter, I am going to explore the relationship between SDG 4 and mental health, emphasizing the transformative potential of Solh Wellness in promoting mental well-being and enhancing educational outcomes.

Correlation of Mental Health, SDG 4 Targets, and Solh Wellness

Target 4.1: Ensure that all girls and boys complete free, equitable, and quality primary and secondary education leading to relevant and Goal-4 effective learning outcomes.

Mental health significantly influences students' ability to access quality education. Mental health challenges can affect students' attendance, concentration, and academic performance.

Solh Wellness offers support in the form of community resources, self help tools, and professional support to address challenges that may impact school attendance and completion rates. This can help reduce absenteeism and improve students' emotional and cognitive intelligence..

Figure 24

Target 4.3: Ensure equal access for all women and men to affordable and quality technical, vocational, and tertiary education, including university

Adding mental health as a part of vocational education can benefit the students to understand their emotions better. This would be a commendable move in guiding kids towards becoming emotionally intelligent, which is an essential skill to have in conjunction with analytical intelligence. Solh Wellness actively collaborates with educational institutions at all levels, addressing the unique mental health needs of girls and boys to advocate access to mental health resources in education. By promoting mental well-being at all levels of education, Solh Wellness contributes to a supportive environment that enables students from all backgrounds to access and benefit from quality education.

Target 4.4: Substantially increase the number of youth and adults who have relevant skills, including technical and vocational skills, for employment, decent jobs, and entrepreneurship

Mental health in itself is a skill - learning coping mechanisms, developing resilience, and becoming emotionally intelligent are all skill sets that help an individual become mentally healthy. Thus, these should be considered as essential outcomes of the educational process which every individual must acquire in order to better tackle problems on a personal as well as professional front. Solh Wellness aims to equip learners with resilience, confidence, and stress management skills that are essential for career readiness and employability.

Target 4.7: By 2030, ensure that all learners acquire the knowledge and skills needed to promote sustainable development

Sustainability is not only limited to the environment, it's about the sustainability of humanity. In this respect, this target can be expanded to include a focus on mental well-being in educational settings in its scope. In turn, this will enhance learners' receptiveness to sustainable development concepts, as well as promote inculcation of mental skill sets into the system which will help in development of a sustainable future. Solh Wellness emphasizes sustainable well-being, empowering learners to engage actively in developing a sustainable mental health for themselves.

Target 4.a: Build and upgrade education facilities that are child, disability and gender sensitive and provide safe, nonviolent, inclusive and effective learning environments for all

There is an immense significance of mental well-being in shaping the overall learning experience, especially when it comes to ensuring active participation and benefits for all. The need is to create safe and inclusive learning environments where neurodiversity is nurtured and every individual can thrive. Solh Wellness recognizes mental well-being as a crucial pillar of inclusive education. We provide resources to manage stress, improve emotional regulation, and enhance coping skills that empower learners of diverse backgrounds to thrive academically and contribute positively to their learning environments.

Conclusion

The intersection between SDG 4 and mental health underscores the significance of prioritizing mental well-being in educational environments. Solh Wellness serves as a powerful tool for addressing mental health challenges, fostering a supportive learning atmosphere, and advancing the key targets within SDG 4. We promote mental well-being, enhancing students' educational experience, foster inclusivity, and prepare learners to become active contributors to sustainable development. Empowering individuals through mental health support and education lays the foundation for a more inclusive, equitable, and prosperous future.

4

Mental Wellness & SDG 5: Gender Equality

SDG 5 (Gender Equality) advocates for equal rights, opportunities, and representation for women and girls across various domains, including education, employment, and decision-making. Mental health plays an important role in achieving gender equality, as societal norms, discrimination, and gender-based violence can have adverse effects on women's mental well-being. If I talk about gender equality, then in my opinion, recognizing and addressing the unique mental health needs of women can help in empowering them to realize their full potential, participate in all spheres of life, and contribute to social and economic development.

Figure 25

Correlation of Mental Health, SDG 5 Targets, and Solh Wellness

Target 5.1: End all forms of discrimination against all women and girls everywhere:

Mental health challenges, such as anxiety, depression, and trauma, can result from gender-based discrimination and violence. Solh Wellness provides a safe and confidential space where women can access mental health support and resources which have been designed to cater to their needs. We offer resources, counseling, and support programs to address women's unique challenges, promoting mental health and wellness.

Target 5.5: Ensure women's full and effective participation and equal opportunities for leadership at all levels of decision-making in political, economic, and public life:

Mental health can influence women's confidence, self-esteem, and assertiveness, impacting their ability to participate in leadership roles. Solh Wellness offers community support to empower women to actively participate in various aspects of life, including education, career, and community engagement. We quest to contribute to women's advancement and representation in decision-making processes.

Target 5.b: Enhance the use of enabling technology, in particular information and communications technology, to promote the empowerment of women

The use of enabling technology, especially information and communications technology (ICT), presents an opportunity to break barriers and create new avenues for women's empowerment. Mental well-being plays a pivotal role in this context, as it significantly influences women's confidence, decision-making abilities, and overall sense of empowerment. Solh Wellness provides resources and exercises to enhance self-esteem and confidence among women. By offering tools for self-affirmation and goal-setting, we help in empowering women to overcome self-doubt and embrace their capabilities fully. We offer content on topics such as maternal mental health, work-life balance, and navigating gender norms, ensuring that women's unique mental health needs are acknowledged and supported.

Conclusion

The nexus between SDG 5 and mental health highlights the importance of addressing gender-specific mental health challenges to advance gender equality. Solh Wellness plays a vital role in promoting women's mental well-being by providing support and empowering women to overcome societal barriers. By offering a safe space, promoting self-care, addressing gender-based violence, and enhancing women's leadership skills, Solh Wellness contributes to the goals of SDG 5 and fosters a more inclusive and equitable society. Empowering women through mental health support and advocacy paves the way not only for greater gender equality but for a sustainable future as well.

5

Mental Wellness & SDG 8: Decent Work & Economic Growth

SDG 8 (Decent Work and Economic Growth) promotes sustained, inclusive, and sustainable economic growth, full and productive employment, and decent work for all. It recognizes the importance of productive and fulfilling work as a fundamental driver of economic growth and social progress. Mental health significantly influences workplace productivity, job satisfaction, and overall economic prosperity. I dive into the relationship between SDG 8 and mental health, with a particular focus on targets 8.5 and 8.8. We can and we should create a conducive environment for economic growth and the well-being of individuals in order to promote a healthy and productive workplace.

Correlation of Mental Health, SDG 8 Targets, and Solh Wellness

Target 8.5: By 2030, achieve full and productive employment and decent work for all women and men, including for young people and persons with disabilities, and equal pay for work of equal value:

Mental health plays a crucial role in achieving full and productive employment. Solh Wellness provides EWP programs and support to enhance mental health literacy and open discussions in workplaces. By creating a supportive culture, we encourage employees to seek help and access mental health resources without fear of judgment.

Figure 26

Target 8.8: Protect labor rights and promote safe and secure working environments for all workers, including migrant workers, in particular women migrants, and those in precarious employment:

An employee faces many issues in professional life, including labor rights that can impact their mental health deeply, especially for migrants and women migrants. We equip employees with self-care tools and emotional support on issues that can impact workplace safety and security. Solh Wellness contributes to healthy work-life balance by focusing on offering a combination of self-help, community and professional support and helping corporates develop structures that are in line with the ideas of giving mental health recognition as a universal human right.

Conclusion

The strong correlation between SDG 8 and mental health highlights the significance of prioritizing workplace mental well-being in promoting economic growth and decent work opportunities. Solh Wellness serves as a powerful tool for addressing mental health challenges, promoting workplace productivity, and advancing the objectives of SDG 8. By providing mental health resources, reducing stigma, and fostering inclusive and safe workplaces, Solh Wellness contributes to the realization of SDG 8 targets. Prioritizing mental health in the workplace creates a positive and productive work environment, benefiting both individuals and society as a whole.

6

Mental Wellness & SDG 10: Reduced Inequalities

The impact of inequalities on mental health is huge. As I see it, perceived discrimination and inequality are perhaps two of the biggest threats to a person's mental well-being. By recognizing the unique mental health needs of diverse individuals and communities, we can strengthen a more inclusive and equitable world. SDG 10 is committed to reducing inequalities within and among countries, ensuring that no one is left behind. Mental health plays a pivotal role in achieving this goal, as it directly impacts individuals' ability to participate fully in society and access opportunities for growth and development. The main target should be addressing mental health challenges to stimulate inclusivity and reducing disparities among diverse populations.

Correlation of Mental Health, SDG 10 Targets, and Solh Wellness

Target 10.a: Implement the principle of special and differential treatment for developing countries, in particular least developed countries, in accordance with World Trade Organization agreements

This target aims to enable special and differential treatments for developing countries, especially the least developed ones so that more progress and development can be done for them. Due to lack of resources, the mental health of these countries is highly affected, which can result in slowed growth in many sectors. Solh Wellness recognizes the mental health challenges that people in developing and least developed countries face due to problems with accessibility, acceptance, availability and affordability of mental health resources. We offer support for coping with stressors and promote emotional well-being by recognizing and tackling these challenges through our sensitization initiatives and free tools and solutions.

Figure 27

7

Mental Wellness & SDG 11: Sustainable Cities and Communities

SDG 11 aims to create sustainable and inclusive cities that prioritize the well-being of their residents. Mental health is an integral component of SDG 11, as urbanization and disasters can significantly impact individuals' mental well-being. Urbanization can lead to increased stress, social isolation, and reduced contact with nature, all of which can negatively impact mental well-being. Cities often face challenges such as overcrowding, pollution, and limited access to green spaces, which can contribute to stress, anxiety, and other mental health issues. Moreover, disasters, both natural and human-made, can have severe and lasting psychological impacts on affected communities, further highlighting the importance of mental well-being for sustainable urban development.

Correlation of Mental Health, SDG 11 Targets, and Solh Wellness

Target 11.5: By 2030, significantly reduce the number of deaths and the number of people affected and substantially decrease the direct economic losses relative to global gross domestic product caused by disasters, including water-related disasters, with a focus on protecting the poor and people in vulnerable situations.

Disasters, whether natural (e.g., floods, earthquakes) or human-made (e.g., industrial accidents, armed conflicts), can have profound psychological effects on individuals and communities. The trauma and loss experienced during disasters can lead to post-traumatic stress disorder (PTSD), depression, and anxiety. Solh Wellness offers resources to build resilience in people suffering from disasters.

Figure 28

Conclusion

Prioritizing mental well-being is not only crucial for individual growth but also for promoting inclusivity and reducing inequalities within our society. Solh Wellness' commitment to addressing diverse mental health needs has played a transformative role in fostering a more inclusive and equitable world. By recognizing and supporting the mental health of diverse communities, we can contribute to the benefits of SDG 10, ensuring that no one is left behind on the path to a better future. As we continue to prioritize mental health and promote inclusivity, we can build a more compassionate and accepting society where everyone has an equal opportunity to thrive.

8

Mental Wellness & SDG 13: Climate Action

SDG 13 aims to take urgent action to combat climate change and its impacts. Mental health is an important aspect of SDG 13, as climate change can have profound psychological effects on individuals and communities. The increasing frequency and intensity of climate-related hazards, such as hurricanes, floods, and wildfires, can lead to trauma, anxiety, and post-traumatic stress disorder (PTSD). The slow-onset impacts of climate change, such as rising sea levels and changing weather patterns, can cause chronic stress and uncertainty about the future, further impacting mental well-being.

Correlation of Mental Health, SDG 13 Targets, and Solh Wellness

Target 13.1: Strengthen resilience and adaptive capacity to climate-related hazards and natural disasters in all countries

Climate-related disasters can result in loss of lives, displacement, and destruction of homes and livelihoods, leading to trauma among affected individuals. Such uncertainties and its potential impacts can contribute to anxiety and feelings of helplessness about the future. Climate-induced migration can also lead to stress, cultural displacement, and difficulties in adapting to new environments, impacting the mental health of affected populations. Solh Wellness empowers individuals to build resilience and adaptive capacity to climate-related hazards. By offering resources for trauma recovery, community support, and disaster preparedness through resilience, we enhance individuals' ability to cope with the challenges posed by climate change. We provide support and resources for individuals and communities affected by climate-induced migration.

Conclusion

SDG 13 and mental health are deeply interconnected, as climate change poses significant challenges to individuals' mental well-being. Solh Wellness has been an invaluable resource in addressing mental health challenges related to climate change and advancing the targets of SDG 13. We provide coping tools for stress, building resilience and adaptive capacity of individuals. We contribute to creating a future where individuals can effectively address the psychological impacts of climate change and build a more sustainable and resilient global community. Together, we can take action on climate change and prioritize mental well-being, paving the way for a more sustainable and emotionally healthy world for generations to come.

Section VI

YOUR MENTAL HEALTH GUIDE

1

Psychotic and Neurotic Disorders: Understanding Common Mental Health Issues

"Wrong solution is no solution, rather a bigger problem."

When it comes to mental health, we often hear specific names like depression, anxiety, or bipolar disorder. But did you know that there are broader categories called psychotic and neurotic disorders? These categories are important because they help us understand different mental health conditions based on their symptoms.

In this chapter, we will explore the basics of psychotic and neurotic disorders. Instead of getting overwhelmed by the specific disorder names, we will focus on understanding the underlying symptoms and how they differ between these categories. By doing so, we can better identify potential symptoms and figure out the right treatment approaches.

Think of this chapter as a guide that will help you navigate the complexities of mental health. By recognizing the fundamental differences between psychotic and neurotic disorders, you'll gain a better understanding of the challenges people face. Armed with this knowledge, you can make informed decisions about how to support and help those who are dealing with these conditions.

Psychotic Disorders

When we use the word "psychotic," it refers to symptoms of a serious mental illness that leads to false belief systems. People experiencing psychotic disorders may feel like their mind is playing tricks on them. They may believe things that are not true, which we call delusions. For example, they might think that someone is trying to harm them or that they have special powers when they actually don't. Their perception of reality can be really strange or not make sense to others.

Another symptom of psychosis is hallucinations. This means that the person sees or hears things that aren't really there. They might hear voices talking to them or see things that nobody else can see. These experiences can be very vivid and real to them, even though they're not happening in the outside world. Additionally, their thinking, speech, and behavior may become disorganized.

Schizophrenia and delusional disorder are two examples of mental illnesses that involve psychosis. Schizophrenia is a long-term condition that affects how a person thinks, behaves, and interacts with others. It can cause a mix of symptoms, including hallucinations and delusions. Delusional disorder, on the other hand, mainly involves having persistent false beliefs without other major psychotic symptoms. Treatment for psychotic disorders usually involves a combination of antipsychotic medication, psychotherapy, and support services.

Neurotic Disorders

"Neurotic" is a term used to describe a mental health condition that involves feeling very anxious or distressed. People with this condition may worry excessively about things that others may not find concerning. Unlike psychotic disorders, people with neurotic disorders maintain contact with reality. Instead, they experience physical symptoms such as sweating, shaking, or feeling nauseous.

Some common examples of neurotic disorders include generalized anxiety disorder, obsessive-compulsive disorder, and post-traumatic stress disorder. Generalized anxiety disorder involves feeling worried or anxious about a wide range of things on most days. Obsessive-compulsive disorder causes repetitive thoughts or behaviors that can interfere with daily life. Post-traumatic stress disorder can occur after experiencing a traumatic event and involves reliving the experience through nightmares or flashbacks.

These conditions can cause significant distress and impact a person's daily life. However, with proper treatment, such as therapy or medication, people can learn to manage their symptoms and live a full life. Treatment for neurotic disorders often involves psychotherapy, such as cognitive-behavioral therapy, medication like antidepressants or anti-anxiety medication, and support services as needed.

It's really important to know that the terms "neurotic" and "psychotic" are not the same and shouldn't be used casually or to judge people with mental health issues. Both conditions can significantly affect a person's ability to function in their daily life.

	Psychotic Disorders	**Neurotic Disorders**
Definition	Disorders characterized by a detachment from reality, involving hallucinations, delusions, and disorganized thinking	Disorders characterized by excessive and maladaptive patterns of thinking, feeling, and behavior
Contact with Reality	Lack of contact with reality	Contact with reality maintained
Severity of Symptoms	Severe symptoms that significantly impair functioning	Symptoms may be distressing but generally allow for functional ability
Hallucinations	Common (e.g., hearing voices or seeing things that are not there)	Rare or absent
Delusions	Common (strongly held false beliefs not based in reality)	Rare or absent
Thought Disorganization	Common (disorganized thinking, speech, or behavior)	Rare or absent
Mood Symptoms	Can be extreme depending on the specific disorder (Bipolar disorder, borderline)	Common (anxiety, depression, irritability)

	Psychotic Disorders	Neurotic Disorders
Examples of Disorders	Schizophrenia, Schizoaffective Disorder, Brief Psychotic Disorder, and Delusional Disorder	Generalized Anxiety Disorder, Obsessive-Compulsive Disorder, Panic Disorder, and Major Depressive Disorder
Treatment Approach	Antipsychotic medication, psychotherapy, and support services as needed	Psychotherapy (e.g., cognitive-behavioral therapy), medication (e.g., antidepressants or anti-anxiety medication), and support services as needed
Impact on Functioning	Significant impairment in daily functioning, including work, relationships, and self-care	Varies depending on the specific disorder, but generally allows for functional ability
Insight into Symptoms	Often lack insight into their condition	Generally have insight into their condition
Who can treat?	Clinical psychologist or Psychiatrist	Most cases can be handled by a clinical or counseling psychologist, but if the situation is serious, a psychiatrist should be consulted.

It's important to note that in treating these disorders, different professionals can provide help. Psychotic disorders are typically treated by clinical psychologists or psychiatrists, while most cases of neurotic disorders can be handled by clinical or counseling psychologists. However, if the situation is serious, it's advisable to consult with a psychiatrist. Both types of disorders require appropriate professional care to support individuals in managing their symptoms and improving their overall well-being.

2

Understanding Therapy and Medication

"Clinical intervention is a must have, albeit only in specific scenarios."

Mental health challenges can be overwhelming, but there is hope and help available. Clinical solutions offer a diverse range of approaches that empower individuals to navigate and transform their lives positively. These solutions are designed to provide support, insight, and healing, ensuring a path to recovery and well-being. Let's explore the key clinical solutions that can make a significant difference in mental health journeys.

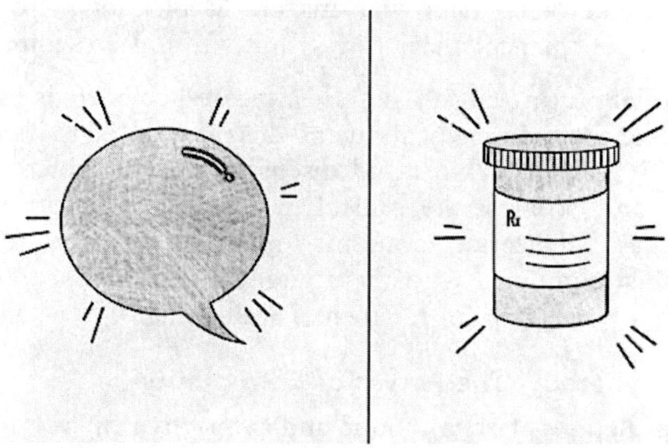

Figure 29

Therapy: Unlocking Insights and Growth

One of the most effective clinical solutions for mental health is therapy. Therapy is a collaborative process between an individual and a mental health professional that can help people understand and manage their mental health challenges. There are many different types of therapy, but some of the most common include:

Cognitive behavioral therapy (CBT): CBT helps people identify and challenge negative thoughts and beliefs that contribute to their mental health challenges.

Dialectical behavior therapy (DBT): DBT is a type of cognitive behavioral therapy that helps people regulate their emotions and develop coping skills through acceptance, mindfulness, and other strategies.

Interpersonal psychotherapy (IPT): IPT helps people understand how their relationships contribute to their mental health challenges and develop skills for improving their relationships.

Medication: Balancing Brain Chemistry

For certain mental health conditions, such as clinical depression, anxiety, and bipolar disorder, medication can play a vital role in recovery. These conditions often involve imbalances in brain chemicals known as neurotransmitters. Medication helps restore the delicate balance, alleviating symptoms and providing relief.

Collaborating closely with healthcare providers is essential in finding the right medication and dosage tailored to individual needs. Regular check-ins and discussions about potential side effects and progress are critical in ensuring the best possible outcomes. Medication alone may not be a complete solution, but when combined with therapy and lifestyle adjustments, it can be a powerful tool for mental well-being.

Group Therapy: The Power of Community

Group therapy offers a unique and supportive environment for individuals facing similar mental health concerns. Participants come together to create a close-knit community where they can share their experiences, offer mutual support, and learn coping skills from one another. The power of shared experiences can be therapeutic in itself, fostering a sense of belonging and understanding.

Group therapy also provides an affordable option compared to individual therapy, making mental health support more accessible to a broader population. Through group interactions, participants develop empathy, compassion, and self-awareness, further enriching their personal growth and resilience.

Hospitalization: A Lifeline in Acute Crises

In severe cases where mental health symptoms require intensive treatment, hospitalization becomes a vital lifeline. Hospital settings offer a structured and safe environment where individuals receive round-the-clock care from dedicated mental health professionals.

Hospitalization aims to stabilize symptoms, ensure safety, and provide access to specialized resources and support. It becomes a pivotal stepping stone towards recovery for those facing acute crisis situations. During hospitalization, clients can receive immediate interventions, medication adjustments, and therapy to address their specific needs.

It's important to work closely with a healthcare provider to find the right clinical solutions for your mental health needs. Mental health conditions vary in severity and causes, so a healthcare provider can help determine the best treatments for you. They can monitor your progress and make adjustments as necessary. By working together, you can find effective solutions and improve your well-being.

3

Who To Call?: Different Professionals and When To Turn To Them

"Choosing an expert is like picking the right playlist for your mood."

Mental health is key to a happy and fulfilling life. But what happens when your mental health takes a turn for the worse? Who do you turn to?

That's where mental wellness professionals come in. These experts are trained to help you with a wide range of mental health issues, from depression and anxiety to substance abuse and PTSD.

In this chapter, we'll take a look at the different types of mental wellness professionals and when to turn to them. So whether you're feeling overwhelmed or just need a little extra support, read on to learn more about how to get the help you need.

Acknowledging and addressing mental health is a sign of strength, not weakness. It takes courage to seek help and work towards emotional well-being.

Profession	Role and Responsibilities	Qualifications	Prescribing Medication	Who can consult?	Common Symptoms?
Psychiatrist	- Diagnosing and treating mental disorders - Prescribing medication - Conducting therapy sessions - Collaborating with other healthcare professionals	- Medical degree (MBBS) - Specialization in psychiatry (MD/DNB)	Yes	A person who has a mental health issue that requires proper diagnosis and medication.	- Symptoms such as hallucinations, delusions, or disorganized thinking. - Self-harming behaviors or suicidal ideation Medication management - Co-occurring mental health and medical conditions - Treatment-resistant mental health symptoms (those mental health symptoms that do not adequately respond to initial treatment or interventions) - Substance abuse and addiction
Psychologist/ Counseling Psychologist	- Studying human behavior, thoughts, and emotions - Providing psychotherapy and counseling - Conducting psychological assessments - Conducting research	- Master's or doctoral degree in psychology	No	A psychologist can be consulted if a person is distressed, nervous, depressed, or needs assistance regarding their work, relationships, or other matters.	- Feeling of loneliness - Mild to moderate depression or anxiety - Stress management and coping skills - Relationship difficulties or family conflicts - Career and vocational concerns - Adjustment to life transitions or major changes - Self-esteem and self-confidence issues - Grief and loss - Personal growth and self-exploration - Communication and interpersonal skills - Lifestyle changes and behavioral modification

Profession	Role and Responsibilities	Qualifications	Prescribing Medication	Who can consult?	Common Symptoms?
Clinical Psychologist	- Assessing, diagnosing, and treating mental health disorders - Providing psychotherapy and counseling - Administering psychological assessments	- Master's degree in Psychology - M.Phil in clinical psychology or Pg Diploma in Clinical Psychology (RCI Registered)	No	A clinical psychologist can handle all cases, from mild to severe. Although, if they feel that treatment requires medications, they refer or seek the help of a psychiatrist. Only a clinical psychologist, in addition to a psychiatrist, can make a diagnosis.	- Severe depression or persistent depressive symptoms - Severe anxiety or panic disorders - Psychotic symptoms, including hallucinations or delusions - Severe mood swings or bipolar disorder - Personality disorders - Eating disorders - Severe trauma-related symptoms or post-traumatic stress disorder (PTSD) - Self-harming behaviors or suicidal ideation - Substance abuse or addiction disorders - obsessive-compulsive behaviors
Counselor	- Offering guidance and support to individuals facing personal challenges - Providing counseling and psychotherapy - Assisting with problem-solving and decision-making	- Master's degree in counseling or a related field	No	Person who is looking for a professional specializing in a particular domain of counseling.	- Career and Educational Counselor - School counselor - Family and marriage Counselor - Relationship Counselor - Special Educator

Profession	Role and Responsibilities	Qualifications	Prescribing Medication	Who can consult?	Common Symptoms?
Psychiatric Nurse	- Assisting psychiatrists and other healthcare professionals in caring for individuals with mental health conditions - Assessing patients' mental health status - Administering medication - Providing counseling and patient education	- Bachelor's degree in nursing - Specialization in psychiatric nursing	No	Psychiatric nurses work at mental health facilities to support psychiatrists in client care.	- Generally Assist psychiatrist in all the symptoms

Profession	Role and Responsibilities	Qualifications	Prescribing Medication	Who can consult?	Common Symptoms?
Social Worker	- Helping individuals and families cope with social, emotional, and environmental challenges - Providing first-aid counseling and support - Connecting clients to resources and services - Advocating for clients' rights and well-being	- Bachelor's or master's degree in social work	No	Anyone who requires assistance, is having social difficulties, or wants guidance regarding locating services can get in touch with a social worker.	- Disability Support - Aging and Geriatric Care - Immigration and Refugee Support - School and Education Support - Child and Family Services - Assistance with housing, healthcare, financial support, and accessing community programs

Your mental health is important. Don't hesitate to seek help from a qualified professional if you're struggling. There are many different types of mental wellness professionals, and each one has their own area of expertise. The right professional can help you get the treatment you need and deserve.

It's also important to remember that you're not alone. Millions of people around the world struggle with mental health problems. There is help available, and you don't have to go through this alone.

So what are you waiting for? Take the first step and reach out for help today. Your mental health is worth it.

4

Neurodiversity and Neuro-Inclusivity

"The toughest challenge or the biggest opportunity - the choice is yours."

The neurodiversity movement emerged in the 1990s with the goal of promoting acceptance and inclusion of all people, embracing their neurological differences. The movement gained momentum as autistic individuals connected through online platforms, forming a self-advocacy movement. Australian sociologist Judy Singer originally coined the term 'neurodiversity' to advocate for equality and inclusion of neurological minorities. People who are 'neurodivergent' have a brain which functions differently compared to the 'neurotypical' population.

Judy Singer saw individuals around her who were being treated harshly because they were neurodivergent. Being neurodivergent herself, and having a neurodivergent daughter, this disturbed her a lot. She wrote her thesis titled " Odd People In: The Birth of Community amongst people on the Autistic Spectrum: A personal exploration of a New Social Movement based on Neurological Diversity", where she discussed how those belonging to the neurodivergent group are treated by society, She also discussed her personal life and how she found out that her own daughter was autistic. Her thesis played a huge role in the campaign for equal treatment for neurodivergent individuals.

Understanding Neurodiversity

People who are neurodivergent are often treated differently because there are multiple misconceptions that revolve around them. To deal with this, the need is to generate awareness and help people understand the concept of neuro inclusivity. Let's start by understanding some basics:

Neurodiversity is not limited to autism: Neurodiversity is a term to describe how people's brains work differently. It's like how some people are good at sports while others are great at art, but being better at sports doesn't make the person superior - both abilities are equally valuable. It includes not just autism but other conditions as well, like dyslexia (difficulty with reading), ADHD (being hyperactive and finding it hard to focus), dyspraxia (trouble with coordination), Tourette's syndrome (having tics or sudden movements), and OCD (obsessive thoughts accompanied by compulsions).

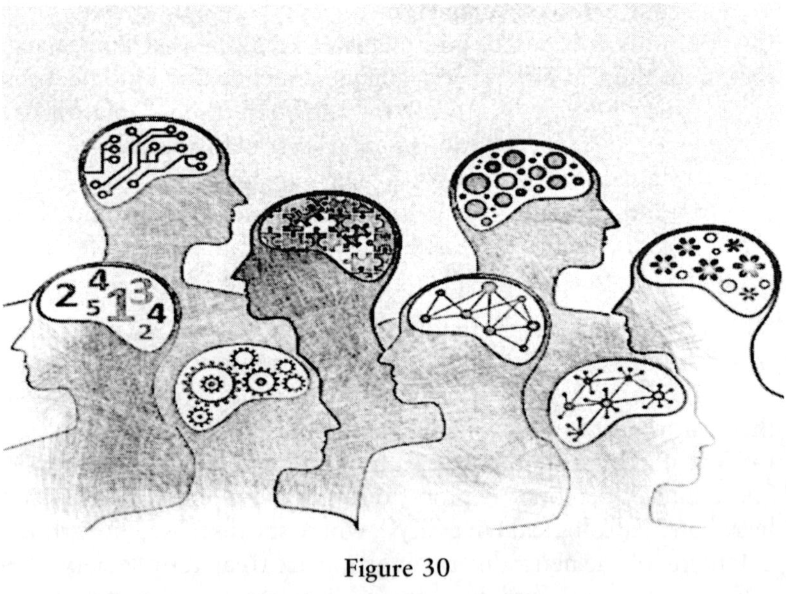

Figure 30

Everyone is unique: Just like no two snowflakes are the same, people with neurodiverse conditions are all different too. Even if they have the same condition, they may be good at different things and find some things more challenging. So, it's important to understand and appreciate each person's strengths and struggles.

Neurodiverse people can do well in work: People with neurodiverse conditions can be really good at their jobs when they get the right help and support. If they have the right tools to do a job well, they can be just as productive and capable as anyone else.

Neurodiversity is not the same as mental health issues: Neurodiversity is about how our brains are wired, like how a computer has different software. Mental health issues are more about how we feel and handle our emotions, like being sad or anxious. They are separate things, even though some people with neurodiversity might also have mental health challenges.

Communication can be different for neurodiverse people: Some people with neurodiverse conditions may communicate in unique ways. For example, they might have trouble picking up on social cues or might be really honest and direct. But that doesn't mean they can't communicate well. It's like speaking different languages; we might just need a little more patience and understanding to communicate.

Neurodiversity is about embracing differences: Neurodiversity is about accepting and celebrating the fact that people's brains work in different and amazing ways. It's like having a big, diverse family with different talents. We should treat everyone with kindness and fairness, making sure they have the same chances to do well in life.

I'm sure by now one thing is clear - neurodiverse individuals are as capable as anyone else. But to be able to hone their abilities, what they need is an environment that allows them to excel. Such is not the case today, because most environments are designed according to neurotypical needs.

So the question arises, how can we create a neuro inclusive environment?

In Schools

- Creating an open and inclusive classroom environment is crucial for engaging neurodiverse students and facilitating their self-confidence. By fostering an atmosphere where questions are welcomed without fear of judgment, barriers to participation and learning are eliminated for these students. Active listening, using both verbal and non-verbal cues, plays a vital role in promoting inclusivity and making students feel valued.

- Recognizing that effective communication is not limited to verbal means, educators should allow neurodiverse students sufficient time to process and express their thoughts in ways they find comfortable. Emphasizing the importance of being true to themselves, teachers can encourage both neurodiverse and neurotypical students to embrace their individuality, thereby building trust and rapport in the classroom.
- To cater to neurodiverse students' unique strengths and weaknesses, educators must take the time to understand their needs and learning profiles. This can be achieved through communication with students, their families, caregivers, and specialists. By implementing diverse teaching strategies tailored to their individualities, lessons become more accessible and effective.
- Presuming competence is essential in avoiding prejudiced assumptions about neurodiverse students' academic abilities. Setting high, yet achievable expectations and providing necessary support and accommodations will empower them to thrive academically and enhance their self-esteem.
- Promoting self-advocacy is crucial for neurodivergent students to express their experiences and learning preferences openly. By actively listening and accommodating their unique requests, educators create a classroom culture of trust and inclusion, where students feel valued and heard in their educational journey.
- Understanding that the classroom is both diverse and neurodiverse, educators can create a supportive environment that fosters inclusivity, removes learning barriers, and empowers students of all types to achieve their potential. By considering neurodiversity when delivering information, planning activities, and assessing learning, educators can cater to the individual capacities of their students, facilitating success and growth for everyone.

In Organizational Settings

- Providing training to all employees and managers on neurodiversity is crucial to breaking down barriers in a neurodiverse workforce. This training should cover understanding the spectrum of neurodiversity, communication styles, and dispelling misconceptions. Managers should also be educated on best practices for accommodating neurodivergent individuals, such as adjustments for sensory sensitivities and extra time for projects. With a better understanding, team members can effectively communicate and collaborate with their neurodiverse colleagues.
- Fostering inclusive recruiting and hiring processes is essential for attracting neurodivergent individuals. Employers can make simple yet impactful changes, such as asking applicants about their accommodation needs during the interview process. Providing accommodations is a requirement of the ADA. Additionally, assessing if social interactions are critical for the position and considering "working interviews" can help evaluate candidates effectively. Employers should prioritize hiring individuals based on their ability to perform the job, rather than how well they fit into social norms.
- Offering flexibility in the workplace is crucial, as neurodivergent employees have individual needs that may require adjustments. Employers should adopt a mindset of flexibility when necessary, using technology and tools like project management software or shared work calendars to assist with prioritization and time management challenges.
- Supporting appropriate socialization is important, recognizing that some neurodivergent individuals may struggle with social interactions. Employers should not base an employee's professional progression on their socializing skills but rather on their contributions to the team and job performance. Optional social opportunities can be provided to allow employees to socialize at their comfort level.
- Seeking help from experts is beneficial in understanding neurodiversity and making necessary adjustments in the

workplace. HR professionals may not have the expertise or capacity to handle such changes alone, so bringing in external consultants or organizations can make a significant difference in creating an inclusive environment.

Conclusion

Practicing neuro inclusivity in both schools and organizations is of utmost importance for fostering environments that embrace diversity, empower individuals, and promote success. By valuing and accommodating diverse neurological profiles, we create inclusive learning and working environments where everyone feels welcome and respected. Neuro inclusivity nurtures creativity, collaboration, and empathy, preparing students and employees to thrive in a diverse world. Moreover, it supports individualized learning and working styles, enhancing academic and professional outcomes. Ultimately, by prioritizing neuro inclusivity, we create spaces where all individuals can reach their full potential and contribute their unique perspectives and strengths, leading to a more inclusive and compassionate society.

5
Exploring Neuro-Developmental Disorders

"Defining and understanding spectrums..."

Autism Spectrum Disorder (ASD)

Have you ever noticed someone who has difficulty interpreting social cues? They may be too loud, too honest, or may seem disinterested in conversations. They may have difficulty moving away from their daily routine, and are extremely sensitive to touch and sounds. These are all symptoms of what we know as autism.

Autistic people are often misunderstood as being rude, or may be marked down as being 'different'. However, autism is not a disease that needs cure, it is something you are born with that makes your brain function in a different way than others. The unique perspectives and way of functioning of autistic people often lands them in trouble with their peers, which is a big reason why understanding the disorder and how it affects daily functioning becomes very important.

What precisely is ASD?

ASD refers to autism spectrum disorder, also known as Autism. It is characterized by a range of social and communication difficulties as well as repetitive and restricted behaviors. The severity of these symptoms can vary among individuals on a continuum (which is why it's called autistic 'spectrum' disorder). Diagnostic criteria for autism allow for identification as early as 18-24 months of age, when distinguishing features become apparent and differentiate it from typical development or other developmental conditions.

The lack of knowledge of ASD in low and middle-income nations may be caused by inadequate information on the condition, a lack of medical professionals with the required training, ignorance of diagnostic resources, and a lack of available public and private funding. In underdeveloped nations, healthcare discourse and research have mostly concentrated on infectious diseases, paying relatively little attention to mental and behavioral problems. The stigma associated with mental health issues and behavioral disorders, particularly in children, has significantly limited the awareness of ASD.

According to a report by ETHealthWorld, about 18 million people in India are diagnosed with autism. About 1 to 1.5 percent of children aged two to nine years are diagnosed with ASD. This statistic goes to show that there is a need to raise awareness about ASD - its prevalence is significant in our country.

Symptoms of ASD

The symptoms of ASD are grouped into two major buckets as per DSM-5, which is considered the golden standard for diagnosis in the world of psychiatry. These are problems in social interactions and showing repetitive behaviors. These symptoms cause significant distress to the individual, and may be accompanied by other characteristics as well. The broad categories of symptoms associated with ASD are discussed below.

Challenges in communication and social interaction: Social communication and interaction skills can be challenging for people with ASD. As a child, autistic individuals may avoid or not keep eye contact or engage in games, not use gestures like waving goodbye, and have difficulty identifying and responding to emotions. Such difficulties persist throughout life in the form of difficulty understanding social cues, not understanding humor or sarcasm, deficits in nonverbal communication, and problems in maintaining relationships .

Restricted Or Repetitive Behaviors Or Interests: People with ASD have behaviors or interests that can seem unusual. These behaviors or interests set ASD apart from conditions defined by problems with social communication and interaction only.

For example, lining up toys or other objects and getting upset when order is changed, repeating words over and over (called echolalia), having obsessive interests in specific subjects, following routines down to the t, flapping hands, and being repulsed by certain textures, sounds and smell.

Other symptoms: Autistic individuals may also show delayed language, movement and learning skills, intellectual deficits, unusual sleeping and eating habits and moods, epilepsy and seizures, and hyperactive, impulsive, and/or inattentive behavior.

Myths and Facts About ASD

Myth: People with Autism Spectrum Disorder (ASD) are intellectually inferior or lack cognitive abilities.

Fact: This is a misconception. Intelligence levels among individuals with ASD vary widely, just like in the general population. While some individuals with ASD may have intellectual disabilities, others may have average or above-average intelligence. It's important to understand that ASD does not determine a person's cognitive abilities.

Myth: Autism is a childhood disorder that individuals grow out of.

Fact: Autism is a lifelong condition. Although early intervention and therapy can greatly support individuals with ASD, it is not something that can be cured or outgrown. However, with appropriate support, individuals with ASD can acquire valuable skills and make progress in various aspects of their lives.

Myth: Vaccines are responsible for causing autism.

Fact: Extensive scientific research has debunked any link between vaccines and autism. Numerous studies have shown that routine childhood vaccinations do not cause ASD. The original study suggesting a connection has been discredited and retracted. Vaccines are safe, vital for preventing serious illnesses, and do not increase the risk of autism.

Myth: All individuals with ASD possess extraordinary talents or savant skills.

Fact: While some individuals with ASD may have exceptional abilities in specific areas like music, art, or mathematics, not all individuals with ASD have savant skills. Only a small percentage of individuals with ASD exhibit these extraordinary talents. Autism is a diverse condition, and the abilities and strengths of individuals with ASD can vary greatly.

Myth: People with ASD lack empathy.

Fact: Individuals with ASD are capable of experiencing and expressing empathy. They may express it differently due to challenges in social communication and interpreting nonverbal cues. Their unique ways of showing empathy, such as practical support or expressing it through their interests, should be recognized and appreciated. By dispelling this myth and embracing diverse forms of empathy, we can foster a more inclusive and understanding society for individuals with ASD.

Undiagnosed ASD

Individuals with undiagnosed Autism Spectrum Disorder (ASD) encounter a range of difficulties that can have significant effects on their daily lives and overall well-being. This includes difficulty in understanding social cues, making it difficult to form and maintain relationships and understand others' perspectives. They may face obstacles in both verbal and nonverbal communication, and have heightened sensitivities to certain sounds, lights, textures, or smells. They may also struggle with planning, organization, problem-solving, and self-regulation. They may also experience challenges in regulating their emotions, leading to intense emotional responses in specific situations. Individuals with undiagnosed ASD are at a higher risk of developing mental health conditions, including anxiety, depression, and low self-esteem. The difficulties they encounter in self-understanding, fitting in socially, and coping with daily demands can contribute to emotional distress.

Obtaining a diagnosis can lead to a better understanding of their difficulties and facilitate access to appropriate support, interventions, and accommodations that can significantly enhance their quality of life and overall well-being.

Management of ASD

As mentioned earlier, ASD is not a disease with a cure. Management approaches vary based on individual needs, with a core objective to minimize symptoms, support development and learning, and enhance overall functioning. Early intervention in the preschool years plays a crucial role in teaching essential social, communication, functional, and behavioral skills. When a child is diagnosed with ASD, it is essential to collaborate with experts to develop a comprehensive treatment plan to ensure that the child's specific needs are addressed effectively.

Treatment options for ASD include:

Behavior and communication therapies: Numerous programs focus on addressing social, language, and behavioral challenges associated with ASD. Some concentrate on reducing problem behaviors and teaching new skills, while others emphasize social interaction and improved communication. Applied behavior analysis (ABA) utilizes a reward-based system to help children learn and apply new skills.

Educational therapies: Structured educational programs tailored to the needs of children with ASD can be highly effective. These programs typically involve a team of specialists and a variety of activities aimed at improving social skills, communication, and behavior. Intensive, individualized behavioral interventions in preschool years often yield positive outcomes.

Family therapies: Parents and family members can learn strategies to engage and interact with their child in ways that promote social skills, manage challenging behaviors, and teach daily living and communication skills.

Other therapies: Additional therapies may be recommended based on the child's requirements. These can include speech therapy to enhance communication skills, occupational therapy to teach activities of daily living, and physical therapy to improve movement and coordination. Psychologists can offer guidance on addressing problem behaviors.

Medications: While no medication can directly improve the core symptoms of ASD, certain medications may help manage specific symptoms. For instance, medications can be prescribed to address hyperactivity, severe behavioral issues, or anxiety.

Learning Disabilities (LD)

Have you ever come across someone in school who consistently spelled words incorrectly despite repeated instructions or someone who struggled with math even though they excelled in other areas? It's highly possible that the child had a learning disability, in its short form, known as LD. Remember Ishan Awasthi from the movie 'Taare Zameen Par'? He had a learning disability which made it difficult to spell words, which we know as dyslexia.

The education system often categorizes students into simplistic labels of "smart" or "dumb," focusing primarily on academic performance. This approach fails to recognize the diverse learning needs and strengths of individuals. It perpetuates a narrow view of intelligence and contributes to the stigmatization and marginalization of students with learning disabilities. Due to this, a child with a learning disability faces many problems in school like inability to perform well in spite of having average or above average intelligence, difficulty in concentration, poor motivation to learn, lack of self-confidence, and low self-esteem.

There is a big need to generate awareness about learning disabilities, because it can easily be understood as a lack of putting in effort by a student, leading to alienation by the comments of teachers as well as sly remarks from fellow peers.

What exactly is a learning disability (LD)?

A learning disability is a neurological condition that affects how individuals process and understand information, learn new skills, and perform certain tasks.

There are different types of learning disabilities, each with its own characteristics and challenges. Some common types of LD include -

1. **Dyslexia:** This is a learning disability that primarily affects reading and language processing skills. Individuals with dyslexia may have difficulty decoding words, recognizing sight words, and comprehending written text.

2. **Dyscalculia:** This learning disability impacts mathematical abilities. Individuals with dyscalculia may struggle with concepts like number sense, arithmetic operations, and problem-solving in mathematics.

3. **Dysgraphia:** Dysgraphia affects writing skills and fine motor coordination. People with dysgraphia may have difficulty with handwriting, organizing thoughts on paper, and expressing themselves in written form.

Attention-Deficit/Hyperactivity Disorder (ADHD) is not a learning disability, but it often coexists with LD. It affects attention, impulse control, and hyperactivity, making it challenging for individuals to stay focused and organized. Other comorbid clinical conditions along with LDs include conduct problems, somatoform disorders, and psychogenic pain like headaches.

Myths and Facts

It is important to dispel some common myths and understand the facts about learning disabilities:

Myth: People with learning disabilities are not intelligent.

Fact: Learning disabilities have no bearing on a person's intelligence. Individuals with LD often have average or above-average intelligence. However, they may face specific challenges in certain areas of learning.

Myth: Children with learning disabilities just need to try harder.

Fact: Learning disabilities are neurologically-based conditions that affect the way individuals process and understand information. Merely exerting more effort may not address the underlying difficulties. Specialized interventions, accommodations, and support are essential to help individuals with LD succeed.

How to help children with LD?

The first and foremost thing that requires focus is the early identification of a learning disability. Parents and teachers play a big role in this context. By being understanding and patient, they can create a supportive environment where children feel safe to express their difficulties and ask for help. Once the LD is recognised, it's all about working to help the child. We need to realize that each child has diverse learning needs and strengths of individuals lie in different areas. LDs can't be cured, thus it's all about figuring out strategies that work best for the child's learning needs and making the necessary accommodations for the same. Some of these are:

Clear Communication: Using clear and simple language when explaining concepts can make it easier for children to understand and grasp new information.

Breaking Tasks into Smaller Steps: Breaking down complex tasks into smaller, manageable steps can make learning more manageable for children with difficulties. Celebrating their progress along the way can boost their confidence.

Multi-Sensory Learning: Engaging multiple senses, such as sight, hearing, and touch, while teaching can enhance understanding and retention of information. Incorporating visual aids, hands-on activities, or interactive materials can be helpful.

Positive Reinforcement: Praising and encouraging children for their efforts and accomplishments, no matter how small, can boost their self-esteem and motivate them to keep trying.

Collaborating with Professionals: Working closely with teachers, specialists, and support staff can ensure that children receive the appropriate interventions and accommodations to help them succeed academically and socially.

Building a Supportive Network: Creating a network of support, including parents, teachers, and peers, can provide ongoing encouragement, advice, and resources for children with learning difficulties.

In conclusion, it is vital to understand and support children with learning disabilities. By promoting awareness, breaking down stereotypes, and fostering an inclusive environment, we can help these children overcome the challenges they face.

Attention Deficit Hyperactivity Disorder (ADHD)

ADHD is a disorder that is in a lot of talk these days and has been a big topic of discussion in the 'relatable memes' culture. This topic attracts interest from many due to the misinformation surrounding it and the recent emergence of cases of adult ADHD. I would say that ADHD is one of the most misunderstood disorders, particularly adult ADHD. Its symptoms are such that it is misdiagnosed very frequently, and the ones who have to bear the brunt of it are those who haven't been able to get diagnosed.

What precisely is ADHD, then?

The full form of ADHD is attention deficit hyperactivity disorder. As the name suggests, it is characterized by a lack of or difficulties in paying attention and hyperactivity. A child with ADHD typically has difficulty sitting still in class, is impatient, impulsive, and often described as 'driven by a motor'. The hyperactivity can also get internalized, which results in racing thoughts that make it difficult to focus.

ADHD is a condition that begins in childhood and can only be diagnosed if its symptoms are present before the age of 18 years. Although some of the symptoms of ADHD can appear in adults as a result of brain damage or other organic causes, one must have had it as a child to be diagnosed with it as an adult. According to the DSM-5 criteria, adults must have experienced multidimensional ADHD symptoms before the age of 12 in order to meet this requirement. If diagnosing in adulthood, clinicians must evaluate both ADHD symptoms that have developed recently and those that have existed throughout childhood.

Adult ADHD symptoms are frequently misdiagnosed by doctors as mood disorders, anxiety disorders, obsessive-compulsive disorder, and other disorders with similar symptoms. Adult hyperactivity may become inward-focused. One might believe that the racing thoughts are a result of anxiousness when, in reality, they might be the result of ADHD-related brain overactivity. It is more challenging to recognize and identify these internal behaviors. Adult ADHD often occurs alongside other psychological conditions, such as anxiety, depression, or substance use disorders. These comorbidities can complicate the diagnostic process and may overshadow the underlying ADHD symptoms, resulting in misdiagnosis.

According to research, between 30 and 70 percent of children with ADHD still exhibit symptoms of the disease as adults. Unfortunately, there is a serious misdiagnosis of adult ADHD. Only 10 to 25 percent of adults with ADHD are properly identified and treated, according to statistics. More than 40% of patients who fit the criteria for adult ADHD in one recent survey were not diagnosed, and only 10% of these adult ADHD patients had gotten any treatment for the illness, despite having seen a healthcare professional within the previous year.

Symptoms during Early Life and School Age

The neurodevelopmental disorder Attention-Deficit/Hyperactivity Disorder (ADHD) is characterized by recurrent patterns of impulsivity, hyperactivity, and inattention that can seriously impair day-to-day functioning. ADHD comes in three primary forms:

Inattentive: People with this form of ADHD suffer from inattention and may find it challenging to maintain focus, pay attention to details, and finish tasks. They could come off as forgetful or disorganized, and they might struggle to stay focused or follow directions. Symptoms include difficulty paying attention to details and sustaining focus, making careless mistakes, getting distracted easily, having trouble staying on track, and avoiding or disliking tasks requiring sustained mental effort.

Hyperactive-Impulsive: The hyperactive-impulsive kind of ADHD is characterized by a person's struggle with impulsivity and hyperactivity. They could come off as nervous and fidgety. Additionally, they might interrupt others, behave impulsively without thinking through consequences, have difficulty engaging in quiet leisure activities, talk excessively and blurt out answers before questions are complete.

Combined: The most typical form of ADHD is the combined kind, which is characterized by both symptoms of inattention and hyperactivity-impulsivity. If a person exhibits a combination of symptoms from both inattentive and hyperactive-impulsive types, they are diagnosed with this kind of ADHD.

Adult ADHD symptoms

Adult ADHD symptoms include trouble starting projects, inconsistent attention to details, issues with self-organization and prioritization, and a lack of persistence in tasks requiring prolonged mental effort. To varied degrees, impulsivity and limited frustration tolerance may be present. Compared to teenage ADHD presentations, hyperactivity tends to be a less prominent symptom in adults. Adults who enter primary care settings may lead chaotic lives, have co-occurring mental health conditions, may appear disorganized, and may depend on drugs and alcohol to "get by."

Adults experience **hyperactivity** more as a general restlessness. This can be seen in difficulty to sit still for long periods of time (through feeling restless at meals, meetings, or movies), talking excessively, or rapidly getting bored after finishing a task. They are always on the go and generally don't respond well to frustrating situations.

Inattentive symptoms in adults are more present in their work or with daily activities of living and present themselves as making careless mistakes, losing things, not paying attention to detail, not being able to follow through with instructions, having difficulty with organization, being forgetful in daily life or they try to multitask without actually completing any of the tasks.

Impulsiveness can manifest itself at work, for example blurting out answers at a meeting, but can also be seen in their spending patterns, engaging in risky behavior, interrupting other people's conversations, making inappropriate comments, intruding upon others, or even monopolizing a conversation.

Debunking Myths about ADHD

Myth: Individuals with ADHD are lazy.

Fact: Neurology plays a significant role in ADHD. Prefrontal cortex development, which is crucial for attention span, planning, and task management, is disrupted which causes problems in following through with tasks.

Myth: ADHD is the result of poor parenting.

Fact: Children that have the disorder are frequently viewed as being terrible kids. But they have a neurological system that is built on interests. As a result, their minds function differently than usual. It has nothing to do with the way one has been raised.

Myths	Facts
ADHD is not a real disorder; it's just an excuse for laziness or lack of discipline.	ADHD is a recognized neurodevelopmental disorder with a biological basis.
ADHD only affects children, and they outgrow it as they become adults.	ADHD can persist into adulthood and affect daily functioning.
ADHD is overdiagnosed, and it's just a result of overactive children being incorrectly labeled.	ADHD is both underdiagnosed and overdiagnosed in some cases.

ADHD is caused by bad parenting or a poor home environment.	ADHD is primarily caused by genetic and neurological factors, not bad parenting.
Medication is the only effective treatment for ADHD.	Medication is one treatment option, but behavioral therapies and lifestyle changes are also effective.
People with ADHD are not as intelligent as those without the disorder.	ADHD does not impact intelligence; individuals with ADHD can have a wide range of intellectual abilities.

Long-term consequences of undiagnosed ADHD

The costs due to untreated adult ADHD are enormous and are associated with greater rates of scholastic underperformance, unemployment, underemployment, divorce, marital separation, substance misuse, cigarette smoking, and automobile accidents.

Untreated ADHD can have a significant, cross-generational impact. Undiagnosed ADHD sufferers may experience difficulties in a variety of spheres of life, which can result in low self-esteem and difficulties in school and at work. To provide appropriate support and therapies for individuals and their families, it is critical to identify and address ADHD.

How Misdiagnosis can be Prevented

Preventing misdiagnosis of ADHD requires a careful and comprehensive evaluation process. It is crucial to conduct a thorough assessment by a qualified healthcare professional specializing in ADHD diagnosis.

This includes considering the diagnostic criteria outlined in the DSM-5 or updated guidelines and ruling out other conditions with similar symptoms. It's important to take into account the person's environment and developmental factors, as well as encourage collaboration among professionals and information sharing. Validated assessment tools should be used to gather objective data, and symptoms should be assessed longitudinally over time. Cultural considerations should also be taken into account.

Promoting ADHD education among professionals and the community can help reduce misconceptions. In cases of uncertainty, seeking a second opinion can provide further clarity. By following these steps, the risk of misdiagnosis can be minimized, ensuring individuals receive appropriate support and treatment.

Management of ADHD

The treatment of ADHD (Attention-Deficit/Hyperactivity Disorder) aims to manage and reduce symptoms to improve daily functioning and overall quality of life. It typically involves a combination of strategies that may include:

Education and Support: Education about ADHD is crucial for both individuals and their families. Understanding the nature of ADHD, its impact on daily life, and available coping strategies can help individuals and their loved ones effectively manage the condition. Support groups or counseling can provide emotional support, guidance, and an opportunity to connect with others who are going through similar experiences.

Lifestyle Adjustments: Certain lifestyle adjustments can help individuals with ADHD better manage their symptoms. These may include establishing structured routines, creating organized environments, breaking tasks into smaller, manageable steps, and using visual aids or reminders. Regular exercise, a balanced diet, and sufficient sleep also contribute to overall well-being and can positively impact ADHD symptoms.

Collaboration and Monitoring: Successful treatment of ADHD requires collaboration between individuals, families, healthcare professionals, and educators. Open communication and regular monitoring of symptoms and progress is important to ensure that treatment strategies are effective and can be adjusted as needed.

Behavioral Therapy: Behavioral therapy is an essential component of ADHD treatment. It involves teaching individuals strategies to manage their symptoms and develop adaptive behaviors. This can include skills training, such as organizational techniques, time management, and problem-solving strategies. Behavioral therapy also focuses on improving communication, social skills, and coping mechanisms. Therapists may work with individuals, families, or in group settings to address specific challenges associated with ADHD.

Medication: Medication is a common treatment option for ADHD. Stimulant medications are often prescribed to help improve attention, reduce impulsivity, and control hyperactivity. Non-stimulant medications may also be used as alternatives or in combination with stimulants. It is important to work closely with a healthcare professional to find the right medication and dosage for each individual.

It's important to note that each person's experience with ADHD is unique, and treatment plans should be tailored to individual needs. Consulting with healthcare professionals who specialize in ADHD can provide personalized guidance and support throughout the treatment.

Conclusion

"It's not about finding 'the one,' but discovering 'the four'."

An arm and a leg for

You must be wondering, "I've just wrapped up this book, and now there is a surprise party going on in my head with all these new concepts on nurturing and sustaining mental wellness, crashing the bash. I'm here, scratching my noggin, thinking, what do I do with these uninvited thoughts and where do I even begin?"

Let me provide you with that. Start with an oddball question: "Would you rather be happy with one arm and one leg or unhappy with both?" It may seem like a peculiar way to start the conclusion of a book on mental health, but bear with me, for it holds the key to understanding the essence of this journey.

Picture yourself at a crossroads, facing this choice. The scenario is designed to make you ponder, to provoke thought about the real importance of mental well-being. What answer could you think of?

"In this era of swiping right and Instagram's ring light, mental health often stays out of sight." But let me take you back to my 16-Hour theory. You need to understand Mental health is the invisible force that guides your every action, influences your relationships, and colors your perception of the world.

Now, let's return to that intriguing question. Would you trade in your brawn for a blissful dawn? It's a question that challenges the very core of our values and beliefs. Some might argue that physical limitations can be overcome with determination and technology, while others might emphasize the importance of happiness, even in the face of adversity. But most of you would choose Happiness. After all, who isn't daydreaming about relocating to Bhutan where Gross National Happiness is the ultimate goal?

The truth is, there's no universally correct reasoning but the assertion is always happiness and peace of mind. Yes, I am talking about the chapter on adjectives. Choosing happiness and peace of mind over the other three adjectives is like picking a sunny day at the beach over a rainy day in traffic. It's just the obvious choice – who wouldn't want to bask in the sunshine of happiness and peace of mind instead of getting soaked in the downpour of sadness, loneliness, and stress? It's not rocket science; it's a simplified science of 5 adjectives by Solh Wellness! Your way of choosing happiness in this hypothetical scenario reflects the uniqueness of your journey towards mental wellness. It illustrates that the path to happiness is not one-size-fits-all; it's a deeply personal and evolving experience. Just as no two people have the exact same fingerprints, no two individuals share identical mental landscapes.

So, even now if you think sustaining mental health is hard and therapy sessions are too costly, only mental health is worth giving an arm-chair and a leg for.

4-People Theory

No mental health discourse is complete without addressing relationships. Allow me to distill four decades of learning into what I call the "Four People Theory." But before that, a little anecdote – one midnight in an elevator, a neighbor asked, "How do you work from 6:30 AM to 12:30 AM?" My initial response: "I love my work." But there's more to it, and it ties into the Four People Theory.

Marriage, once a vital institution, now often feels antiquated. In the 21st century, women's independence means they no longer require the traditional support structure that marriage provided. So, what's the modern role of marriage? In my view, it should solve four problems:

Figure 31

1. **Day-to-Day Companion:** Someone to share everyday moments with.
2. **Soulmate:** A partner to share life's ups and downs, dreams, and secrets.
3. **Long-Term Partner:** A companion to grow old with.
4. **Fuck Buddy:** Fulfillment of physical desires.

The catch? These roles may not necessarily be fulfilled by one person. Attempting to force-fit all these needs onto a single relationship often leads to dissatisfaction, divorce, and emotional turmoil.

Marriage today should be seen as any other friendship. Just as you don't panic when a friend can't go out partying with you, you shouldn't expect your spouse to fulfill every role. And these relationships need not adhere to traditional gender norms or sexual orientations – diversity is the norm in our modern world.

This evolution has given rise to diverse relationships and convenience marriages, not just in wedlock but in all kinds of relationships. Marriage as an institution isn't inherently flawed; it has simply lost its relevance and requires reform.

So, I urge you to assess your relationships and consider if change is needed. The Four People Theory presents a practical framework for understanding and nurturing these connections. Personally, I advocate for non-exclusive, open relationships to embrace the full spectrum of human connections while honoring personal growth and freedom. It's a perspective I've lived by, and it has allowed me to be there for friends when they need me while maintaining the autonomy to prioritize my life as I see fit.

Food Security

Picture this: a future where we've all become a little more self-sufficient. I'm not just talking about growing a pot of basil on your windowsill; I'm envisioning a world where we produce a significant portion of our own food. It's a future where we're not solely reliant on external sources for sustenance, especially those uncertain supply chains that can cause so much anxiety. In this future, knowing that I can grow a variety of fruits, vegetables, and herbs in my backyard or on my rooftop gives me a sense of security. It's like a safety net for my pantry, and it significantly lowers my stress levels. After all, who wouldn't feel better knowing they have a hand in putting food on the table?

But it's not just about being self-sufficient; it's about doing it sustainably. Imagine a world where our agriculture is powered by solar energy and smart technologies that minimize waste and environmental impact. When we can see our food supply as stable and environmentally friendly, it eases a different kind of anxiety—ecological anxiety. We're less worried about food scarcity due to climate change or other environmental factors. We feel more at peace with the planet, and that peace translates into a sense of psychological comfort.

In this future I'm painting for you, we've also shifted our priorities. We've moved away from the relentless pursuit of material possessions and status symbols. It's a back-to-basics lifestyle where we value community, our connection to nature, and our own self-sufficiency. This kind of simplicity can work wonders for our mental health. We're less consumed by the pressures of consumerism, and our minds are free to focus on what truly matters.

Now, let's talk about something a bit heavier. In this same future, we're living in a world where the stakes are higher than ever before. We're aware that a single individual or a small group could possess the power to trigger global catastrophe. It's an existential threat unlike anything humanity has faced. It's a pivotal point, a moment in time when we, as humans, find ourselves in a truly unique and precarious position. For the first time ever, we have the capability to destroy everything we've built, to unravel the tapestry of our existence.

There's something else that sets it apart from any other point in human history. Think about it: throughout history, even in the darkest times, there was a limit to the scale of destruction a single human or group of humans could unleash. Take Hitler, for instance. He wrought havoc on a global scale, causing immense suffering and devastation, but he couldn't destroy the entire world. No fascist leader, no dictator, no matter how tyrannical, possessed the means to wipe out all of humanity.

But now, because of the advances in technology, because of the development of nuclear, biological, and chemical weapons, that limit has been shattered. The power to obliterate everything we know and love is within our grasp. It's a sobering realization, isn't it?

As you close this book and embark on your own unique journey, I want you to carry with you the understanding that mental wellness is not a fixed state. It's a continuous process of self-discovery and growth. Just as our bodies require daily care, our minds also need nurturing. So, my dear reader, as you move forward, remember that it's okay to ask for help when you need it. It's okay to take a step back and prioritize your mental health. It's okay to embrace imperfection and recognize that life's challenges are opportunities for growth.

The Solh Revolution: Mental Health for All

Linking the themes of "An arm and a leg for," the "4-People Theory," and "Food Security" to Solh Wellness, we find a common thread of prioritizing well-being and balance in our lives. Just as one might contemplate the value of happiness when faced with a choice involving physical sacrifice, Solh Wellness encourages us to prioritize mental well-being, even in a world often preoccupied with external appearances and material success. The "4-People Theory" underscores the importance of diverse and fulfilling relationships, mirroring the need for community support in the Solh Wellness framework. And as we envision a future where self-sufficiency and sustainable living alleviate anxiety, it resonates with Solh Wellness's emphasis on holistic well-being. In essence, Solh Wellness serves as a compass guiding us towards a life where mental health, relationships, and sustainability are cherished. Picture this: You're standing at the crossroads of life, and in front of you is the majestic signpost called Solh Wellness. It points in three promising directions: Self-Help, Community Support, and Expert Intervention. You can either pick a lane and stick to it or be the adventurous mental health road-tripper, switching directions on a whim!

Self-Help Tools: It's like having your very own Doraemon, always ready to pull out the perfect tool to tackle any emotional hurdle! You can assess yourself, set goals, analyze your mood, and dive into a library of knowledge. It's like having a personal therapist in your pocket, minus the awkward silences.

Community Support: Ever wished for a judgment-free zone where you can pour out your thoughts and feelings? Well, Solh Wellness has it. Anonymity? Check. A journal for your innermost thoughts? Check. Support groups and a Solh Buddy to guide you through it all? Double check. It's like having a secret society, where instead of secret codes, you share your deepest feelings and thoughts openly.

Expert Services: Sometimes, you need a mental health lifeguard, and Solh Wellness provides just that. From clinical interventions to allied therapies, it's like having a mental health lifeline on speed dial. Need to talk to someone right now? You got it. Need a tailored mental health package? Consider it done.

With these tools at your disposal, you're not just a passenger on the journey to better mental health; you're the captain of your own ship. And if you ever feel lost at sea, Solh Wellness is there to rescue you.

Solh Wellness is not just an app; it's a movement, a revolution that aims to break down the barriers and shatter the stigmas surrounding mental health. We're not here to create quick fixes; we're here to lay the foundation for lasting mental wellness.

Think of us as mental health architects, designing a world where mental well-being is as important as breathing, where seeking help is a sign of strength, not weakness. We're in this for the long haul, because real change takes time, effort, and genuine commitment.

The 4Cs of Mental Health

In life's puzzle, the 4Cs are four crucial pieces – Climate, Contagion, Conflict, and Conformity. They all contribute to the bigger picture, much like essential elements in a complex equation.

Climate: Just like the weather, life can be unpredictable. But with the right mental wellness tools, you can weather any storm.

Contagion: Sometimes, emotions are contagious too. One person's positivity can spread like wildfire, while negativity can infect a whole room. Be the spark that lights up the room.

Conflict: Even life is a battle, and sometimes, the toughest wars are fought within. But armed with the tools of Solh Wellness, you can conquer your inner demons and emerge victorious.

Conformity: In a world of trends and expectations, it's easy to lose yourself. But remember, true mental wellness means being authentically you, regardless of what's trending.

Mental Wellness and the SDGs: A Global Connection

Mental health isn't just about individual well-being; it's woven into the fabric of global progress. The Sustainable Development Goals (SDGs) and mental health are like two sides of the same coin.

Imagine a world where all the SDGs are achieved – poverty eradicated, gender equality realized, climate action taken, and so on. But if people are still struggling with their mental health, have we truly achieved anything?

Solh Wellness stands at the intersection of the SDGs and mental health, ready to bridge the gap between individual well-being and global progress. We recognize that mental well-being is not just a goal in itself but a catalyst for achieving all other goals.

In the end, let's embrace the wisdom of Mann and Demann, follow the rhythm of the 5 adjectives, and embark on the Solh Revolution – a journey towards a world where mental wellness is not just a goal but a way of life.

As we come to the final lines, let's make a fun pact, you and I. Should this book take the world by storm, I promise not to let it "go to my head." Instead, I'll ensure it stays right where it should. After all, that's where all the best conversations with imaginary penguins and debates with inner critics happen – "In my head." I appreciate your company on this mind-bending journey, and I'd like to remind myself and everyone else that the best approach is to stay grounded and embrace the delightful chaos that's constantly brewing up there.

The End... or rather, The Beginning.

About the Author

Kapil Gupta is the founder of *Solh Wellness*, a mental wellness platform offering free tools for individual mental health management and comprehensive solutions for organizations. With a mission to enhance mental well-being, Kapil has successfully introduced his innovative mental health approach to over 30 organizations, engaging with thousands of users in the process.

In addition to his focus on mental health, Kapil is a versatile entrepreneur, founding *OMLogic*, *PragatiE*, and *Frontlist*. As the digital editor of *Global Dialogue Review*, a foreign affairs magazine, he contributes to international discourse. Kapil is also a co-author of the book *India Vision–New Age Equality* (2021). Renowned as a compelling speaker, Kapil has addressed prestigious conferences like SMX Singapore, Social India Conference, OSI Days, Engage 2012, and OMCAR. His expertise extends to mainstream media platforms such as Republic TV, CNBC Awaaz, and BBC World, where he has provided commentary on diverse subjects including social media, social change, and foreign affairs.